THE FIFTH VICTIM

Antonia Alexander

THE FIFTH VICTIM

MARY KELLY WAS MURDERED BY
JACK THE RIPPER NOW HER GREAT GREAT
GRANDDAUGHTER REVEALS THE TRUE
STORY OF WHAT REALLY HAPPENDED

JOHN BLAKE

Published by John Blake Publishing Ltd,
3 Bramber Court, 2 Bramber Road,
London W14 9PB, England

www.johnblakepublishing.co.uk

www.facebook.com/Johnblakepub **facebook**
twitter.com/johnblakepub **twitter**

First published in paperback in 2013

ISBN: 978-1-78219-441-5

British Library Cataloguing-in-Publication Data:

A catalogue record for this book is available from the British Library.

Design by www.envydesign.co.uk

Printed in Great Britain by CPI Group (UK) Ltd

1 3 5 7 9 10 8 6 4 2

Papers used by John Blake Publishing are natural, recyclable products
made from wood grown in sustainable forests. The manufacturing processes conform to
the environmental regulations of the country of origin.

Every attempt has been made to contact the relevant copyright-holders,
but some were unobtainable. We would be grateful if the
appropriate people could contact us.

This book is dedicated to my family for all their
support and invaluable information, and to the two
Mary Kellys, whose trials and tribulations gave me
the premise for this story.

Thanks to my family and friends for their patience.
To my agent Cate Lewis for her help and understanding, and to
Allie Collins, Clare Tillyer, Liz Mallett and all the team at John
Blake for making this book possible.

CONTENTS

CHAPTER ONE   1

CHAPTER TWO   13

CHAPTER THREE   27

CHAPTER FOUR   47

CHAPTER FIVE   53

CHAPTER SIX   71

CHAPTER SEVEN   81

CHAPTER EIGHT   101

CHAPTER NINE   127

CHAPTER TEN   147

CHAPTER ELEVEN   161

CHAPTER TWELVE   181

CHAPTER THIRTEEN   189

CHAPTER ONE

Heavy rain began to fall again; I looked out of my window at the relentless downpour pounding the pavements below. I'd heard on the news that this was the worse June in history for rain, hey but look on the bright side, the hosepipe ban had been lifted, unlike my spirits.

I had had a phone call from Nan, she lived in La Cala and I hadn't visited for a while, but she wasn't her usual cheerful self; she might be 81 but her wicked sense of humour and her positive outlook on life made everyone around her feel good. I could feel something was worrying her so I offered to go over to see her; knowing I apportioned my time with university and my family she usually told me to wait until the holidays to visit, but this time she immediately said: 'Yes love that would be great'.

I was instantly worried, although I'd asked her a number of times she kept insisting everything was fine, but there was always a 'but, I'd love to see you'. I told her I would come over as soon as I could arrange a flight.

I needed to speak to Philip, my husband, I knew he was due some time off and I wanted him to take it to look after Lana and Maddie, our two daughters; I didn't want to take them on this trip, I sensed something was wrong and thought it would be better to see Nan by myself.

I had been married for five years now and although juggling family life with University was difficult at times I wouldn't change it. I loved being a wife and mother; I remember the night I had met Philip.

It was the hen night of one of my best friends, Jessica. I always took ages deciding what to wear on a night out and this night was no exception. I finally decided on a snug-fitting black halter neck dress which I felt very sexy in. I could hear a car horn beeping outside signalling the arrival of my taxi.

Stepping into the cab I was greeted by Emily, my oldest friend and confidant; we had gone to primary school together, then comprehensive, then college and now University. Emily had arranged the hen party and was her usual boisterous happy self as I took a seat in the cab.

'Wow Tonia, you look great!' she squealed, hugging me to her ample bosom; all my close friends and family called me Tonia, all except for my Dad who always called me Antonia.

I returned Emily's compliment, 'Thanks, so do you.'

And she did with her blonde, not-a-strand-out-of-place hair, low-cut red top and black pencil skirt. She has the looks a lot of girls would be envious of.

We had arranged to meet the others at a club; Emily had been there on numerous occasions and had guaranteed us all a great night. We headed down the stairs of the club, receiving admiring looks from some of the male staff and customers; I hadn't been out socially for a long while, so I was unused to such attention and I could feel myself blush. The room was smaller than I imagined, but I liked it. There was a cosy feeling with candlelit tables around the dance floor, stools placed discreetly at each corner, and a friendly-sounding DJ churning out all the latest chart hits.

'Over there, look,' Emily shouted above the noise. 'The others.'

Emily pulled me by the arm towards a table just ahead of us. I was looking forward to the evening, it was the first time in over a year that we'd all got together, and we all got on really well despite being very different characters. There was Jessica, the bride to be, a petite blonde, who had been with her fiancée since she was 18; she was always quiet and unassuming. Then there was Brooke – a very giggly, happy-go-lucky girl, curvaceous with long, dark-brown hair. And then there was Ebony – the serious one who went out even less than me. Tall and very elegant, she has strawberry-blonde hair and the most amazing green eyes.

Emily and I ordered some drinks; the others looked as if they'd had a few already. After a lot of talking and some more drinks we were all ready to take to the dance floor.

'Come on, girls!' shouted Emily. 'Let's go show 'em what we're made of.'

Although I rarely went to clubs, I loved to dance; I was convinced that dancing around the house to the radio or the music channel was what kept me in shape. We were all having a great time. Even Ebony had loosened up and was shaking herself around as much as the rest of us.

'Wahoo!' Jessica screamed above the noise of the music. 'I'm having the best time.'

'We should do this more often!' admitted Brooke.

'Well, it's not like I haven't tried.' Emily's I-told-you-so tone left us in no doubt.

After what seemed like an eternity on the dance floor, I went back and sat down at the table. Emily and Ebony kept dancing while Brooke took Jessica to the toilet. The 'hen' was beginning to look a little the worse for drink and quite unsteady on her feet. I looked around at my fellow clubbers. Some obviously made this a weekly visit, while others looked a bit out of place.

I called out to a passing waitress. 'Excuse me; can I

get some drinks, please? Two Bacardi and diet cokes, a vodka and lemonade, glass of white wine and a soda water with lime.'

Soda and lime seemed a good option for Jessica. She'd need to sober up a bit if she was to enjoy the rest of her night. Still dancing, Emily edged closer to the table, then bent down to speak, as quietly as the club's noise allowed, into my ear.

'Don't look now, but you've got an admirer. Over by the bar.'

Feeling a little self-conscious, I took a sneaky look anyway. Sure enough there was a guy looking at me. I turned away quickly, but knew he was still staring. I turned to look again.

'Oh my God!' I said, panicking. 'He's coming over.'

I couldn't help but look at the good-looking dark haired man approaching me. I gulped as he smiled – it made him look even more gorgeous – and I found myself grinning back.

'Hi! I hope you don't mind me coming over. I knew you'd seen me looking at you and, rather than just sit there staring and probably spooking you out, I thought I'd just come and say hello!'

'No, I don't mind. And hello to you too.'

He seemed relieved that I hadn't told him where to go; he sat himself on the seat next to me and held out his hand.

'I'm Philip.'

'Antonia.' I replied returning the courtesy.

'Ooooh!'

We both turned to my friends grinning at us, and I waved them away like a pack of giggling schoolgirls.

'Sorry, I don't want to interrupt your party,' he said.

'No no, you're not,' I said reassuring him with a smile.

It was the usual small talk at first – names, jobs, where we lived. But, before we knew it, we were talking about dreams and ambitions – the conversation flowed so easily. I hadn't felt this good in a long while. He stood up to order us both another drink – I didn't mind, anything to prolong our time together.

I discovered through our conversation that Philip was a chef at an expensive restaurant nearby; needless to say I hadn't been in there too often, just when it was a special occasion and my dad was paying. Being a student I couldn't yet enjoy the finer things in life; Mum would always tell me…'all your hard work will pay off in the end,' but until that time arrived I could always depend on the bank of dad.

I was studying medicine and it would be a while yet before I would start to make any money; I loved what I was doing though, it was hard work, and you had to be committed. Half of my class had dropped out already, but I was going to see it through until the end. That was the main reason I hadn't been out socialising;

my university work was time consuming. The last thing I was looking for was a relationship, but something told me that Philip was different and I felt an instant bond with him.

We looked around and the club was starting to empty. My friends signalled from across the room that they were ready to leave.

'I'd better be going.' I said apologetically and reluctantly.

As I stood up, he caught me by the hand.

'Do you have plans for tomorrow?' He looked a little embarrassed. 'I'd like to see you again.'

Being a Sunday, it was the only day I relaxed: dinner with mum and dad and then just lounging around watching TV.

'Well, nothing much.' I shrugged, trying not to look too eager.

'Would you like to come out for lunch, with me, and maybe a walk after?'

I didn't need to think for too long. 'Sounds good.' I smiled, slipping away from his grasp. I had already exchanged numbers with him.

'Ring me in the morning and we'll make arrangements.'

'OK.' He said smiling, 'see you tomorrow.'

Just over an hour later I lay in bed, excited at the prospect of seeing Philip again. I'd never felt so comfortable with a man I'd just met. I couldn't believe the things I'd told him about myself, my dreams and ambitions.

After talking on the phone for over 15 minutes the next morning, we made plans for him to pick me up at my flat and then head down towards the Mumbles for some lunch. I was so nervous; I kept looking out of the window in eager anticipation and a little trepidation. What if it didn't go as smoothly as it did last night, what if he didn't like what he saw in the cold light of day…without the ambiance of dimmed lighting and candles, would he still find me as appealing?

I was about to find out; I saw a car pull up outside and Philip get out. He was just as good looking as I remembered…even more so. He looked cool and relaxed in his faded blue jeans and dark blue shirt. He looked up and saw me at the window, I jumped back nervously, I grabbed my bag and made my way out… checking my reflexion in the mirror as I did.

He kissed me gently on the cheek when I reached the car, and the hairs on the back of my neck stood up. It felt good and I wanted to kiss him back. He opened the car door for me and I got into the passenger seat. I needn't have worried; we talked as though we'd known each other for years, we were so at ease with each other and I found out that we had loads in common, not least our sense of humour.

We didn't end up going to Mumbles, we headed instead towards Gower, it was a lovely day and what better place to go than to the Gower Peninsula, renowned as the first place in Britain to be designated an area of outstanding natural beauty.

After lunch we just walked, talking and laughing constantly. I was falling for him; everything felt so right, this wasn't like me at all, I was always sensible and level headed. My head was saying 'get a grip, you hardly know this guy'…but all my other senses were telling me otherwise.

We sat on an embankment and he kissed me passionately. All reasoning went out the window as I kissed him back, we lay back on the grass not saying anything, he took my hand and we lay there in silence looking up at the sky. The sky was completely blue – no shades, no hesitations or doubts, just endlessly, solidly blue. Yet as I stared up at it I couldn't find the source of the blueness – the part where the world ended and heaven began. I remember staring for so long that my point of view changed and I felt as though I was looking down from the sky at myself – a dun-coloured dot, insignificant yet surrounded by the most breath-taking scenery.

The months that followed were blissful; Philip was everything I wanted. My parents, however, were not so thrilled. We got engaged after six months and Phil was seven years my senior, but I wanted to spend every waking hour with him. I fell pregnant soon after our engagement; we didn't plan it but were thrilled nevertheless. Mum and Dad had come around, I knew they only wanted what was best for me and this wasn't how they had envisaged my future. Mum was great with my pregnancy, making sure I ate well and looked after myself...unfortunately I lost the baby at four months; we were all devastated.

We had planned to get married abroad after the baby was born, but after the loss Phil and I became closer than ever and decided to bring the wedding forward and two months later we were married in the Greek island of Lindos. It was a small affair, just close family and friends, and I couldn't have wished for a better day. The ceremony took place in the hotel grounds and I felt like a princess, all the guests were out clapping and there were utters of 'bellisimo' and 'bella, bella'. Not long after we returned home I discovered I was pregnant again; I had conceived while on honeymoon. We were over the moon. I put university on hold and concentrated on the pregnancy... I wasn't going to lose this one, I don't think I could have coped with another loss. Thankfully, I didn't have to.

Our daughter Lana finally arrived; it was a magical day. I remember looking at her, checking she had all her fingers and toes, as you do, and thinking what a miracle creating life was. Philip and I couldn't take our eyes off her she was so perfect, she was also so big 8lb 14oz, and had a mop of black hair. My parents couldn't believe their eyes when they saw her; not only did she look exactly like I did at birth, she also weighed the same.

I had planned to go back to university, but I didn't want to leave the baby it didn't feel right. I wanted to focus on her; I think losing a baby made me more protective.

Two and a half years later our little Maddie joined the family, another 'mini me', I was told. And six months later I decided it was time to go back to university, Mum said she would look after the girls, which would make things a lot easier. I felt guilty leaving them, but I knew I needed to make something of my life if I was to help them make something of theirs.

Now, had I forgotten to pack anything? I walked around the house I'd been renting for the past three years checking I had everything. The house was Victorian, most of the original features had been taken out when the owners had refurbished it. The two bedrooms, large bathroom and living/kitchen area were all we needed for the time being, although we had talked of maybe getting something a little bigger.

I kissed the girls and told them to be good for their dad, though I knew they'd run him ragged. Kissing Phil, I made my way to the taxi that was waiting outside.

I was all set; my flight left from Cardiff at 6.30 in the

evening, the airport was relatively quiet which is why I liked using this airport; it was unlike Gatwick or Heathrow which would have been bustling with throngs of people trying to find their check-in desks. Cardiff airport is very small in comparison with just a handful of check in desks, some car rental companies and a help desk on the ground floor and first floor, toilets, a couple of eateries and an amusement arcade section. I checked in and made my way through to the departures where I browsed through the usual airport shops before making my way to the VIP lounge situated at the back of the departures. I had a free lounge pass which allowed me six visits courtesy of my bank and I must say it came in very handy, especially as I was travelling alone. I sat next to the window that overlooked the runway sipping my vodka and Diet Coke and nibbling on my bowl of veggie crisps thinking, what was it that was worrying my Nan so much?

The flight was on time and just two hours later we had landed. As I descended the steps of the plane I looked up at clear blue skies, and inhaled the warm fresh air deeply. I felt physically lighter, my stress already lifting, the warmth of the sun gently caressing my skin.

CHAPTER TWO

I picked up my bag from the carousel and made my way out of arrivals; I climbed into a taxi and sat back, a little relieved to be away from the hustle and bustle of the chaos that is my life. It seemed strange to be here without the family, especially the girls. By now I'd usually be trying to placate and cajole the girls into behaving themselves, although they were very good generally; I think when they're so young the travelling makes them a little stir crazy.

Looking out of the window I took in the view of a mixture of villas to one side and land that had been untouched by time, no buildings, just the perfect emptiness covered by a vast blue sky. The taxi swerved quickly to avoid two young boys bouncing along on a motorbike, their shirts open and blowing in the wind;

the taxi driver just shrugged his shoulders and smiled at me in the rear view mirror.

After about an hour we pulled up outside Nan's villa; she had lived there for about 20 years, when the area was unspoilt by high-rise apartments. The villa was close to the sea but the view had long been blocked out by the large buildings.

As I approached the gate Nan was heading out to meet me, she never ceased to amaze me, she was elegant and still a very attractive woman. She was strong and independent and had the most wicked smile.

We hugged and she led me into the villa, the smell of baking filled my nostrils and I knew that it was the gym again when I returned home.

'How are the kids? Why didn't you fetch them with you?'

'I thought it would be nice just to a have a bit of you and me time', I said trying to sound convincing, not wanting her to sense my concern.

I put my case into my room and returned to the kitchen just in time to be presented with a cup of tea and a slice of Victoria sponge.

Sitting at the table I noticed that Nan wasn't her usual chatty self.

'You OK Nan?'

'Yes love I'm fine, I've got something I want to talk to you about though.' I was intrigued.

'I'll be right back' she said as she walked out of the kitchen.

I sat waiting, looking around at my cosy surroundings. The table was covered with a gingham cloth, and a teapot complete with cosy sat in the centre of the table along with the sugar. The fridge freezer was encased with magnets, gifts from family and friends from all over the world. Her Rayburn six-ringed cooker had seen better days but Nan wouldn't use anything else, it had served her well and I had the sponge to prove it. I was still sitting there swathed in the warmth of the room when Nan came back in, carrying a magazine and an old decorative box, which she placed on the table.

'I have a few things to show you; but first read this.' She handed me the magazine, which was in Spanish.

'Nan you know I can't read Spanish.'

'All these years you've visited me, you should have learnt the language by now.'

I knew she was right but in my formative years while visiting her all I wanted to do was have fun and go to the beach.

Nan took the magazine back, tutting her annoyance.

'*Mas Alla* is a sort of investigative magazine, it covers various articles, concerning things like religious miracles, UFOs and unsolved mysteries. I read it now and again. David Benito, a Spanish boy, a very good investigative reporter, did a story on some man from

Wales who has written a book about a relative of his, who he's convinced is Jack the Ripper.'

I was confused, what did that have to do with my Nan, and why was it upsetting her so? She then handed me two sheets of A4 paper which were tucked inside the magazine,

'Here, you can read this first, it's been translated. It's another article by David Benito concerning the same story.'

'I don't understand Nan, what....'

'Just read it love.'

I started to read the article, entitled 'Prologo Jack el destripador'.

Practically since I was a kid, I stalled deep in the figure as one of the most soulless beings in history. Books, films, radio programs, documentaries...all trying to find one of the great enigmas that have raised more hypotheses to throughout history: the identity of 'Jack the Ripper.' There are places, historical figures and events which, despite the years, still emerging information try – although in most cases remains in attempt, solve enigmatic events. Come to my head 'Roswell case', the Nazca lines, the Kennedy assassination...or many other issues, although there will be new information, will always remain under discussion and is the perfect breeding ground for the emergence of new hypotheses. The identity is hidden behind the considered most famous mass murderer in history, I thought that since the murders were committed in 1888, the investigation was improperly by the police and little evidence could have come down to us to solve the case, this matter would be another of many who would, year after year, creating new stories that never lead to the resolution of the case and yes to the constant speculation. And you may encounter new information, but none is so revealing and clarifying like everything compiled in the book they have in their hands and, dare I say, this is more serious research on the Ripper resolutive.

During my visit to London, how could it be otherwise, I did not miss the opportunity to know the exact places where the famous Victorian murderer carried out the brutal crimes. While it is true that some areas have little to do with the 19th century, there are certain points that, doing a little exercise of imagination, we move mentally and try to reconstruct what happened in the, by then, reviled neighbourhood Whitechapel. In its streets, imagining some of his dark and hidden passageways without a hint of light, one is able to see Jack, the poor prostitutes who were murdered, the police evidence eliminating erroneous result of research, poor people wandering the neighbourhood and frightened men and women before the appearance of that human monster capable of biasing life without a shred of compassion. As I say, all this having been reported previously, it is difficult to 'see' in situ. But you, dear reader, I appreciate what you have in your hands. Thanks to all the information you are about to read, not only can do that *I destrito* visual tour, but you can also put a face, name the famous Jack the Ripper.

You, unlike what happened to me, you can reconstruct the murders trying to figure out Jack's gesture while he killed his first victim, how was the fateful and accurate movement of his hands holding a knife to an expert in surgery and obstetrics, the point where they could escape, where he worked, what connection had with their victims, that is, can know fairly accurately all matters relating to, until now-not-now-mysterious face that was hidden behind the top hat, an elegant coat, a briefcase full of gadgets surgery and a horse-drawn carriage.

And you, as I do these bold and strong statements, you may wonder why I'm so convinced. To clarify this issue, just say that Tony Williams, a researcher and author of this book presents a large number of tests. And when I say I do not mean testing hypotheses that further increase the legend of Jack.

Tony had no interest in the figure of Jack, or even knew in depth the details of the murders. But as a result of trying to understand and deepen the life of one of its most prestigious ancestors in medicine Victorian society came to treat the royal family, was found with the surprising and unpleasant discovery that their ancestor 'Uncle' John Williams, who could be hiding behind the Whitechapel murders. Since then, there have been many hours of research trying to see if his suspicions were groundless. And finally, microscopic crystals with traces of uterine tissue, a myriad of written documents, testimonies, a mysterious knife, a newspaper trying to hide information from the time of the murders, the real motives for the killings, theorizing with a lot of sense…there are many tests that Tony Williams brings to settle the case that many students of criminology and mystery lovers would like to solve.

If someone knew that an ancestor was in times past, a ruthless murderer, would you have the courage to take all this information to light? Would it be able to tell though created conflicts in its own family? Are you willing to dethrone someone considered almost as a hero when he finally was not so? For Tony Williams has done so and is the reason because I feel obliged to make known this story, so far limited to British readers.

Probably will not see Jack as 'the goose that lays the golden eggs,' but it is. That's why many are against this brave work. It is much better, I checked myself, continue speculating the impossible identities, coaxing tourists to do tours of the most important places related with Jack and finalize the photographs showing the multiple identities that they could hide behind murderer. There are many who are interested in having never known the truth about this case because, otherwise, would not give so many benefits. But the reality is different and you are about to discover it. I'm proud that some insignificant letters written by someone who always wanted to know who hid behind Jack, preceding the final work to put an identity to anyone in 1888 who was able, or even of suspicion. Say the book in your hands is the book I always wanted to read About Jack the Ripper, i.e. a dream come true. Now if I can say loud and clear: 'CASE SOLVED'.
David Benito

'What's this about Nan; it's not making any sense. Since when have you been interested in Jack the Ripper?'

'I'm not love, but this story has pulled us into the centre of these horrible murders.'

Now I was completely puzzled...was my grandmother going senile, she was talking and acting bizarrely and I was getting worried.

'Nan', I tried to reason, 'It's just a story, nothing to do with us; we're not mentioned in the magazine are we?'

'It's not only the story, it's the picture…look at it.'

Again I looked at the magazine, not knowing why. There was an old black and white photo of a man, probably middle aged, with receding hair. I was just about to say something when Nan handed me an old silver locket.

'Look at it,' she said, thrusting it into my hand.

'It's lovely Nan, I haven't seen this before.'

'It was my great grandmother's, look inside.'

I opened it up and inside was a picture of a man, the same man that appeared in the magazine; younger but it was the same man.

'Is this your great grandfather?'

'I thought it was until I saw this article, my great grandfather's name was George.'

'Perhaps you got the name wrong, perhaps it was John.'

'No, I've got the family tree. And besides, this all fits in with the stories I've been told.'

Now I was intrigued, where was all this going?

'I'll tell you everything tomorrow love; you must be tired, I know I am. Get some rest and we'll talk in the morning.'

My curiosity had been tweaked – how was I supposed sleep? But Nan looked exhausted so I said nothing, except goodnight.

I lay on my bed looking up at the ceiling fan rotating; the breeze it gave was cool and welcoming on this hot and humid night…although it had seen better days and also gave off a whine, which was annoying to say the least. My mind was racing; I was thinking of all the various scenarios of what Nan was going to tell me…was her great grandmother mad? Was this doctor part of our family? Eventually I gave in to my mind's exhaustion.

When I went down stairs the next morning Nan was in the garden. I looked at her through the kitchen window; she was pottering about pulling up some weeds. She looked preoccupied, I'd never seen her like this before, it was as if she was on autopilot. Did she sleep at all last night, I wondered, seeing how tired she looked. I went to the door and called to her:

'Nan, do you want a cup of tea?'

'Oh yes please love, I'll be in soon.'

I put out the cups and poured the boiling water into the teapot, leaving it to steep, Nan liked her tea nice and strong. As I was putting some toast into the toaster Nan walked in, kissing me on the cheek.

'Good morning love did you sleep well?'

'Yes, fine' I lied.

'I'll just go and wash my hands then and we can have breakfast.'

I had just finished putting everything out, including her homemade jam and marmalade when Nan came back in. We sat down and ate in relative peace, I wanted to ask her what was on her mind, but I could see she was mulling things over in her head and she would tell me in her own good time. Then she broke the silence.

'How are you're studies going?'

'They're OK, glad to get away for a while though.'

'Yes, Mum and Dad said you'd been working hard. It's a pity they can't come over at the moment, it would have been nice seeing you all together.'

'Mmm' was all I said, thinking one person fussing was enough, three didn't bear thinking about. Being an only child wasn't all it was cracked up to be; I'm not complaining, it also had its advantages too…but it was the overprotectiveness, little things like not being able to catch the school bus with the others, or being driven to and from school or anywhere else I needed to go to. Mum was afraid something bad would happen to me and Dad was just Dad, doing whatever was needed to keep the peace.

After breakfast I cleared everything away, I could see Nan taking some paperwork out of one of the drawers; she laid them out neatly on the table, she sat down tapping the chair next to her for me to do the same. She seemed to be thinking for a minute before saying:

'I'm going to tell you a story I was told by my grandmother. We were a close family…all from the heart of Swansea. My grandmother was a very homely person, she always said how much I looked like her mother, Mary, with my long dark hair and fair complexion. When I was about your age she told me about her mother and the doctor she met, John Williams, he was handsome to her, she said, and very different to her father, who worked in the ironworks. She was used to hard working, hard drinking men who always looked grubby and expected everything done for them. This doctor, however, was educated, charming and clean, he was a far cry from her father and Mary liked that. She didn't enjoy the life she was living; she wanted better.'

'She first saw the doctor outside his surgery, which wasn't far from where she lived. She asked him if he had any work going for her, he didn't have anything but was impressed not only by her looks, she was a very beautiful girl, but also by the fluent Welsh she spoke. Over a short period of time they became quite close; they enjoyed each other's company. Mary was in love, but life moved fast and the doctor was an ambitious man and Swansea didn't have the opportunities he craved. He got a position at a hospital in London; Mary was devastated, London couldn't be further away for someone like her…a working class girl who never travelled anywhere. But not only that, what she also found out was that not only was he moving away, he was to marry, not to her but to the daughter of a rich factory owner. In fact he owned the ironworks her father worked at.'

'Apparently his prospects were better if he was married, and as much as he thought of Mary, she and her family couldn't get John where he wanted to go; he needed someone with means. He told Mary that he loved her but this was the way things had to be for now, she was heartbroken, and unfortunately she still loved him. He promised he would visit as often as possible. Time passed and Mary was giving up hope of seeing John again; she started to see a man from the ironworks, your great grandfather, a quiet and gentle man who was besotted with her. They married soon after meeting and Mary became pregnant quite quickly, they were happy together, looking forward to the arrival of the baby and settling into married life. After their baby daughter was born they became closer as a couple; it wasn't the life she saw for herself but Mary was content, she had a beautiful healthy baby and a husband that really loved and cared for her, everyone said she looked radiant and happy. A few years passed and they had a couple more children. Then everything changed; she heard from John, he was in Swansea and wanted to see her. She felt guilty but agreed.'

'He'd come back to visit family and friends, and although they were both married now, he still wanted to see her. Why couldn't he have just left things alone? My mum said the family were upset and tried to reason with her but she wouldn't listen. She continued to see him behind her husband's back but it wasn't long before the rumours circled back to him. He must have obviously been angry; who wouldn't have been? Not only do you find out your wife is having an affair, which is bad enough, but how could he compete with a rich doctor who could afford to give his wife the life he could never provide for her?'

'When John returned to London he must have arranged for Mary to follow him, because not long after she left Swansea and her family and travelled to London.'

CHAPTER THREE

The feeling that I had discovered something that I was not meant to lingered with me for the next few days. It made it harder to have a normal conversation with my family; at first, I did not want to tell even my husband, Philip, what I had learned. But eventually the information I had bottled up inside me had to come out. Not only did I need to tell him what I had found out, I also needed to have someone question it. If he was convinced by my argument, then perhaps I would be convinced as well. Or perhaps I wanted to poke holes in my findings; perhaps I wanted to be proved wrong. If so, I was wasting my time. Philip was shocked at first, but then became as carried away by the story as I had been. Neither of us knew much about the Jack the Ripper killings but we made it our business to find out. We read an array of paperbacks from our local library; and nothing we read contradicted what little I knew about it. But we also came up against a new problem; we now knew a lot about the Ripper, but comparatively very little about my relative.

I thought about what I knew from Nan, and what she had told me about the man Mary had supposedly had an affair with. I thought that if Mary had some kind of secret life, my first step must be to uncover something about it, and maybe that would shed more light on whether or not my suspicions had any foundation. I needed to find out exactly who this man was, and whether or not there could be any link to my relative. But how to go about this? Although I had spent time researching subjects before, those were fairly easy tasks; the books were in the library, nobody had anything to hide, it was all reasonably straightforward to put together. This was going to be very different; I would have to work hard to find the information I needed, and nowhere would this be more true than within my own family.

Did my mother know anything about the story of Mary and if she did why hadn't she mentioned it before? Thinking about it, if it wasn't for the new evidence about this Sir John Williams being Jack the Ripper, then there wouldn't be much of a story to tell. I needed to find out all I could about this man and the link he had with my great great grandmother.

My first duty was to ask Tony Williams for information relating to his ancestor. He was very helpful and emailed me tons of data, telling me I could use what I wanted from it. There was so much; where did I start? The beginning would be good, I thought.

John Williams was born on 6 November 1840, in Beili, Gwynfe, his mother's family home, before being carried back to his family's farm, Blaen Llynant, in Llangadog in Carmarthenshire in rural Wales. His mother, Elinor, already had two sons, David and Morgan; she subsequently had a fourth, Nathaniel. Her only daughter, Elizabeth, died aged two and a half, barely three months after John was born. John's younger brother, Nathaniel, was the last of the line, as his father, David, died of typhoid fever when John was only two. John's birth was registered nearly a month after his birth, on 5 December, indicating that he was a healthy enough child. He certainly appeared healthy during his long life, living as he did until 1926, when he was aged 86.

The farm nestled on a hillside in the north-west of the Brecon Beacons, hidden from the valley below, and at the time John Williams was there consisted of a solidly built farmhouse where the family, their servants and farmhands, together with the local schoolmaster, lived; and a variety of outbuildings.

Nowadays those outbuildings are cottages available

for rent; the Big Barn is large enough to 'accommodate [a] string quartet for dinner'. Years ago, before the farm buildings had been converted, the yard would have looked very different from the smart and peaceful scene it is now. The day-to-day activity of the place, and the mess that would have gone with it all, have been replaced by a sloping lawn, tranquillity and ordered beauty.

John Williams's early life would have been part of this living farm and the rural activities that went with it. The farm had been managed by the family with the aid of a couple of farmhands, so it would have been a busy place, demanding of the time the residents of the farm could spare. Even the young John Williams would have found plenty of work for himself, with chores to be done both before and after school.

Elinor appeared to expect the very best from her sons and servants. The boys were taught to believe in a strict God, and this belief was rigidly enforced. Perhaps she felt she had to make up for the loss of their father. Not only did she teach her children to read and write in both Welsh and English, the servants were taught too – something that her neighbours regarded with suspicion, as an affectation of a woman trying to rise above her circumstances.

In those days women were not yet allowed to own property. The Married Women's Property Act had not yet come into force, and it was only when it did, in 1870, that the laws regarding ownership of the home allowed married women to be on equal terms with men. So the suspicions of her neighbours might also have been heightened by their sense that she was herself slightly over-reaching her station in running a farm in the first place. Especially so when it turned out that she could run the farm better than many of the men who lived nearby, and that her farm became something of a model one in the area.

The best sources of information about John Williams's early life are two books: one written in Welsh about their mother, by John's younger brother Nathaniel; the other, written by Ruth Evans about John Williams himself, and published in both Welsh and English by the University of Wales Press at the behest of the National Library. Nathaniel's book was printed after her death – apparently paid for by John Williams – and runs to about 90 pages. It is a small book, with less than 170 words on every page. The frontispiece carries a photograph of Mrs Elinor Williams – a forbidding-looking woman, stern and unyielding in her gaze.

The fact that John lived a life so far removed from the rural farm of his childhood, with his houses in London, and his work for the royal family, shows that while Elinor was able to provide her sons with tremendous self-confidence she was not able to encourage more than one of them to follow in her footsteps. It is interesting that John and his older brother fled the maternal nest when they could: John to London and Morgan as far as the United States in order to do so. David, the eldest, stayed to work on the farm but he died when John was 22, and it was left to the younger son, Nathaniel, to work alongside his mother, tied to her apron strings. Nathaniel stayed on the farm until he died in 1908, 18 years before his older brother John, at the age of only 65.

The real detail of John's childhood comes from a speech he made, when he was 60 years old, to the new intake of medical students at the University College of South Wales and Monmouthshire. In it he suggests much about his daily life as a small boy, although he does so in a roundabout way, referring to himself in the third person. We know from this speech, and from the few other sources left to us, that he was lively, outgoing and resourceful as a boy; but there is no hint in the boy's life of what was to come. We know that he was very fit, for he frequently refers to this in later life, certain that his health in his middle and old age stemmed from the daily exercise he had taken as a boy. We know he did not consider a career as a doctor until he was quite a lot older, and he appears to have been quite happy to have accepted the future his mother had devised for him as a minister. We know that on more than one occasion he addressed the congregation at the local chapel, where his father, David, had been the minister.

In the absence of her husband, Elinor Williams was a woman of high standards and high expectations. She 'was one of those rare women whose courage and faith never failed her and who, even when faced with sorrow and disaster, always found salvation in hard work,' said Ruth Evans. It sounds as if she were much like her more famous son – easy to admire for some, difficult to love for everyone. Nathaniel's book records her working tirelessly in the farm during the day and then sitting up into the night, reading voraciously. Sadly, we do not know what it was that she read so enthusiastically, but we can be sure it was of a religious bent. She lent horses, carts, farm hands and her own eldest son to help build the new Capel Maen Congregational Chapel in 1852, and then moved her family there to worship, abandoning the Reverend D. Jones's Chapel of Bethlehem. It was in this chapel that her son John first preached.

John Williams was probably no different from most boys. He walked to school, as we know for he tells us so often; the walk to the local school was three miles each way, and John Williams treasured this time not only for the love of healthy exercise it bred in him but also for the opportunity it gave him to explore the natural world. 'I confess that I look back upon this period of my life not only as one of the pleasantest and brightest but also as one of the best spent, for the effects have been my mainstay during the rest of my career,' he told the medical students of Monmouthshire in 1900. He continued:

Children had to walk to school from one to three miles in the morning and home again in the evening, carrying with them their midday meal. To accomplish this distance a boy took from an hour and a half to two hours in the morning. He reached the schoolroom at 9 o'clock and was supposed to work until 12 o'clock. Then followed a relaxation from work lasting two hours, a few minutes of which was occupied in partaking of a very simple meal, but a meal which was consumed with a relish and an enjoyment which many a luxurious epicure would give all but his dinner to possess.

This meal, frugal as it was, was ample for the child's requirements. Then came the great pleasure of the day, hockey, football, or hare and hounds (cricket was unknown in country schools in those days), than which no exercises, games or gymnastics are better calculated. Thoroughly refreshed and untouched by fatigue the boy entered school again at 2 o'clock and remained until 4 o'clock. Then came the journey home, which occupied in winter at least two or three hours and in summer from three to four, with all its delightful incidents, un-beclouded by the thought of a home task [homework] – a new imposition condemned by every healthy-minded boy. The boy never took the straight path or the shortest route. His curiosity, his inclination, his spontaneous energy, call it what you will, led him to deviate to the right and to the left from the normal course. He, moreover, required amusement and play after his exhausting labours in the schoolroom. There were various objects of interest which had to be visited on the way home. In a pool a mile up the stream on the left was the old trout, which had to be tickled or presented with various cunningly-devised invitations to land, to which his wariness never condescended to reply. On the right was the track of a hare. This had to be carefully inspected, while the discovery of a gin was a source of intense enjoyment and the division of its string afforded a doubly exquisite pleasure, for it ensured puss a free run and baulked the cunning and skilful poacher in his nefarious designs. Then the nest of an old crow upon a high and solitary tree should not be forgotten. It was some distance off, it is true, but it demanded a daily visit in the spring of the year, and the strongest and bravest boys climbed up in turn to inspect and count the eggs and in the end generally to rob the nest. This would sometimes lead to a falling-out – an event which is said to happen rarely among thieves, but in this instance the honest bird did not come by its own. The encounter took some time to come to an issue. Unfortunately the morning told the story of the evening and this led to the application of the appropriate but unpleasant remedy.

Parts of the idyllic portrait of his youth reveal something of the man in the boy. Ruth Evans, who after all is kindly disposed to the subject of her book, writes that, as the leader of his little pack of friends, John Williams would assume lordly command over his fellows, and 'with sly persuasion' would get them not only to carry his satchel and books back for him, but 'sometimes even himself on their backs, when walking became a trifle irksome'.

He later transferred from the local school in the Ceidrych valley to the Normal School in Swansea. His friends there, who went with him from Gwynfe, included Esay Owen, who was to marry Annie Roberts, the girl in the nearby farm to the Williams's. Annie Roberts – always close to John Williams as a child, and as far as John was concerned it was to him she would be married – was also related to him, according to Ruth Evans. The farm, which in the same area as the Williams farm in Gwynfe, was called Glantowy, and covered over 160 acres.

The school that John Williams travelled to in Swansea was originally meant for teachers, to prepare them for their careers. While at the school, the young man continued to preach at the local chapel. But it was the head of the Normal School, Dr Evan Davies, who encouraged his interest in the natural world and the sciences, and it was here that John Williams deviated from the path his mother intended for him.

Elinor Williams had wanted her son to take a career in the ministry, and everything in his life so far had been geared towards that. Apart from the influence of Dr Davies, though, it is hard to know what persuaded him to stand up to his formidable mother. One thing is sure, though; John Williams was brought up by his mother to think quite highly of himself. She gave him an enormous sense of his own self-worth; a confidence which enabled him to leave her and head for Scotland, and a year's study of mathematics at the university in Glasgow. Later in life John Williams acknowledged that neither he nor his mother knew what he was going to do after that, though he knew enough by then to know that his future did not lie in the chapels of Wales. 'Certain I am, however, that neither my mother, who was my guide, nor I myself had worked out any positive scheme or definite plan as to the future of my education, nor as to my business in life.'

John Williams must have enjoyed his time in Glasgow.

He kept his lecture notes and all these years later they can still be read in the archives of the National Library of Wales. The first outside account of him came from his teacher, Professor Blackburn, who wrote a report on the year he spent there. It tells us that he attended classes with 'unfailing regularity', that in his exams he answered 'extremely well', his conduct in class was 'excellent', and his exercises 'admirable'. He won second prize for 'general excellence', as voted for by his classmates, and his professor thought this something to which he was 'fully entitled'.

What does all this tell us so far? John Williams was physically strong, naturally curious, determined, ambitious, used to assuming a position of pre-eminence among his peers, hardworking, successful academically if not outstanding at this point; in short, he possessed many of the characteristics that we would see later on in his working and private life.

I can understand, now reading about him, what my great grandmother saw in this man. He was probably everything her husband wasn't and, judging by what Nan had told me of her, she was his female counterpart, feisty, strong willed and determined. She knew what she wanted and if she had been born into a rich or middle class background she would have got it.

My great grandfather on the other hand was happy

with his lot, he must have known, however, that his wife was not; he knew she wanted more than he could give her and what was tragic is that he knew that she loved someone else who could give her the life she desired. The one thing he did have though was something John Williams would never have – children, someone to carry on the lineage…

After his year in Stanhope Street, John Williams returned to Wales and very quickly decided on his future. Perhaps something happened in Glasgow to clarify matters for him. There were no doctors in the immediate family, so it is hard to know where the impulse came from. Perhaps he was influenced by a family friend; perhaps something he had learnt at school aroused his curiosity. Clearly he wanted to do something other than go into the ministry; and when he returned home in July 1859 he took up the first post in his long medical career, as an apprentice to two Swansea general practitioners, Dr Ebenezer Davies, who had trained at Guy's Hospital in London, and Dr W. Henry Michael, who had lately been the Officer for Health in Swansea. Maybe it was thanks to the enthusiasm of Dr Davies, or perhaps it was already in John Williams's mind, but after he had worked for two years as apprentice to the two doctors, he moved to London to continue his medical career there.

John Williams was a supremely confident man; although he came from a small Welsh valley, he and his brothers were encouraged by their mother to feel they could accomplish anything they set their minds to, and London cannot have seemed such an extraordinary choice for the young man. After all, his elder brother Morgan was already in the United States, where, in just a few years from then, he would join up with the Heavy Artillery Regiment of New York and fight on the Union side in the American Civil War. With that example in mind, London cannot have seemed so very far away to the 21-year-old John Williams. Ambition was something that he shared with Morgan, but it seemed to have eluded their younger brother, Nathaniel, who was content to remain at his mother's side till she died.

In December 1861 John Williams started his formal training at University College Hospital in Gower Street in London, where he was a remarkably successful student. What was London like when John Williams arrived? The city then was not the extraordinary capital of the empire it later became at the height of Victoria's reign, when a doctor was a significant figure in society; it was still a city in transition. Refugees in their thousands from Eastern Europe were entering the capital. Although the Metropolitan underground railway had been opened, most transport was by horse, whether in a carriage or a horse-drawn omnibus. The sewage system had yet to be properly established – the vast underground constructions that still function as London's sewers, and which shifted the filth from the streets, were only completed by the end of the decade. But the visitor to London would have marvelled at the scale of everything around him – whether it was the size of the buildings or the numbers of people living among them. 'The visitor who finds himself for the first time on London Bridge is distracted by the rush of life, the noise of wheels, the trampling of horses, and the murmur of myriads of voices, and other confused sounds, that seem to fill the air,' wrote the *Cassell's Illustrated Guide to London* for 1862. The guide's writers feel impelled to tell us, with the kind of efficient Victorian bureaucracy that we were coming to know so well, that 107,000 people used the bridge every day, and that 20,000 vehicles crossed it as well. They go on: 'But the order that prevails in all this confusion is greater than the din of business, and soon makes itself felt. In a few moments, the most unsophisticated rustic will acquire perfect confidence, feeling that it is no turbulent crowd, but an ordered march of intelligent beings, of which he finds himself a part.'

We know enough about John Williams to know that he would not have considered himself an 'unsophisticated rustic', but nevertheless he would have been impressed by the view from London Bridge.

Towering above the city was St Paul's Cathedral, but it was not alone on the skyline – many of today's sights were there as well. The monument to the Great Fire of London, Mansion House, Westminster Abbey, the Houses of Parliament, Lambeth Palace – all of these would have been sights for the young John Williams to see on his arrival in the capital.

As well as the churches no doubt prescribed by his mother, the young Welsh student would have visited the musical halls, the theatres, and other places of entertainment. Perhaps he would have ventured a little further afield. The *Cassell's Guide* does not cover Whitechapel, but it leads the reader through the docks (so that it was possible to witness London's vibrant trade with the world) and only here mentions one of the downsides to London: the whores, or 'drabs', on the lookout for sailors ready to spend their wages. Here too, we are told, 'gin and beer in this region dispute the possession of our olefactories with tar'.

Little is known about John Williams's time in London when he was a student. University College Hospital was his main base, but records of where he lived while he worked at the hospital are nowhere to be found.

He studied the following: anatomy (with dissections); physiology (including general physiology and morbid anatomy); chemistry; practical chemistry; *Materia Medica* (essentially, the branch of medicine to do with preparing and using drugs); botany; forensic medicine; theory and practice of medicine; theory and practice of surgery; midwifery; and hospital practice. He was a conscientious and hard-working student, and when he finally became a doctor he carried with him medals and certificates to show that he had been one of the best candidates of his year.

'Listerism', named after its chief practitioner, Dr Joseph Lister, was making its appearance while John Williams was studying. This innovation involved the use of antiseptics to help prevent the spread of infection during and after an operation. Before this time, the most trivial operation was likely to be followed by infection, and death occurred in up to 50 per cent of all surgical cases. A review of hospitals published in 1894 stated that, during the late 1860s and throughout the 1870s, when John Williams was right in the midst of this time of change and progress, hospitals were 'places which healthy people should avoid and sick people should shun,' because of the risk of infection there. After Louis Pasteur discovered that bacteria caused fermentation, Lister realized in 1865 that the formation of pus was also due to germs. At first, he used carbolic acid sprays to kill germs in the air, but later he realized that germs were also carried by the surgeon's hands and instruments. He insisted on the use of antiseptics on hands, instruments, dressings, and on the patient.

Later on in his career, Williams assiduously followed the use of these antiseptic practices within his chosen field, obstetrics, but to have practised them in his student days would have been nothing less than revolutionary. Some of his contemporaries still felt that boiled water and speed were the prerequisites of a successful operation. That many doctors resisted the use of antiseptics seems bizarre.

To his contemporaries, John Williams was therefore something of an innovator, recalled today for his 'pioneering work' in abdominal operations as an obstetrician. John Williams had been trained by doctors who had themselves learned their trade in the mid-19th century, with the values and expectations of that age. So the way the medical profession developed during those decades is relevant in the sense that the principles John Williams adopted were learned in those classrooms and surgeries. He might well have learned from these men as much as from teachers such as Lister.

He was awarded many prizes: in 1862, a silver medal for chemistry; in 1863, one for anatomy and physiology; and, chief among these, in 1864, a gold medal for pathological anatomy. The medal was made of gold, and, when he married a few years later, he punched out some of the gold to melt into a ring for his wife, which he fashioned himself. Also in 1864, when he was made assistant to the Obstetric Physician at UCH, he began working in the area of medicine that was to consume all his later life. He achieved his first medical qualification, Licentiate of the Apothecaries' Society (LSA) in 1865; this enabled him to take up a post as house surgeon in University College. He moved to Brompton Hospital and then to Great Ormond Street Hospital for Sick Children, during which time he qualified as a member of the Royal College of Surgeons (1866) and became a Bachelor of Medicine. In the following year, he finally achieved his aim of becoming Doctor of Medicine. He must have enjoyed living in London, and certainly he knew that if he were to fulfil his ambitions, it would be in London hospitals. It is unlikely that his mother felt the same; doubtless she had brought him up to speak both English and Welsh because she wanted her son to contribute to the life and culture of Wales. Through the library he more than fulfilled her aim, but everything indicates that she would have liked him to return to Wales as soon as he had completed his studies in London and to set up in practice in Wales.

CHAPTER FOUR

At this point, things stopped going his way for the boy from rural Wales. Instead of staying on the path recommended for aspiring young doctors – that is, to take a job at a hospital in London and learn his profession there – he returned to Swansea to become a general practitioner. Perhaps John Williams felt he owed his mother a duty of care for the sacrifices she had made so that he could travel to Glasgow and London to study. Living and studying in London cannot have been cheap, especially when compared to rural Wales; his board and lodging had come part and parcel with University College Hospital, but his mother had paid for her son's other expenses, as well as the cost of tuition, amounting to what would have been between £73 and £105 a year, with books, instruments, examination and registration fees on top.

Or was this his first professional setback? Despite his outstanding career as a student, John Williams failed to be taken on at any of the London hospitals where he had trained, and he returned to Swansea to seek work not within a large teaching hospital but as a general practitioner. Perhaps he regretted his choice of specialisation, although it would have been possible to further his interest in obstetric medicine – defined as 'medical care in pregnancy and childbirth' – within the confines of his practice.

So either Williams turned his back on London or it turned its back on him. John Williams would have to live in Swansea, and work there for some years, before he would be welcomed back.

While John Williams had been away in London, his old employer in Swansea, Dr W. Henry Michael, had retired. Dr Michael's position had been taken instead by Dr Davies – the practice was now known as Davies and Davies. Dr Andrew Davies had previously been a surgeon in the coalmines of Wales, working for the Golynos and Varteg Iron and Coal Works. Dr Ebenezer Davies had taken up another role as well; he was also Admiralty Surgeon and Agent. Shortly after John Williams returned from London, Davies and Davies moved, and Dr Ebenezer Davies changed jobs once again, this time becoming Medical Officer for Health in Swansea. John Williams returned and gradually took over the patients of his former employers; they moved on, with Dr Andrew Davies moving west from Swansea to become a surgeon at the Cardiff Infirmary, later known as the Cardiff Hospital. John Williams set up his practice in 10 Heathfield Street. He proudly displayed his credentials so that his new patients would know that this was not the apprentice of former days, but a fully-fledged London doctor who they were dealing with. If John Williams found it depressing to return to Wales – qualified to work in a major hospital but instead finding himself treating patients out of a house in a small street in Swansea – there was also another huge disappointment awaiting him. The woman he had wanted to marry had married his best friend while he was away in London. Annie Roberts had chosen Esay Owen over John Williams, and this left him alone amidst the circle of friends he had made in Swansea earlier.

Back in Swansea in the late 1860s, John Williams may have felt isolated by Annie's change of heart and his friend Esay's marriage to a woman he had regarded as special to him. And so while he would have spent time with new acquaintances discussing Welsh culture and walking the hills around Swansea, he would certainly have found time to see his former employer, Dr Ebenezer Davies and his new partner, Dr Andrew Davies. Perhaps John Williams would have asked them for help in establishing himself in practice in Swansea. In any event, in under a year he had moved to 13 Craddock Street and there he practised until 1872. While he worked there, he also took on other employments, perhaps learning from the Drs Davies; in the early 1870s he became the Medical Officer of the Post Office in Swansea (a job that Ebenezer took over after John left Swansea). Dr Andrew Davies, meanwhile, after some time as President of the Swansea and Monmouthshire Medical Association, a society that John Williams would have belonged to, left the partnership with Dr Ebenezer Davies, and retired to Cardiff.

John Williams quickly established himself within the professional world in Swansea. He joined societies, such as the local medical ones, and he also joined the Freemasons. The Freemasons have long had their name associated with the Jack the Ripper crimes, but there is nothing in John Williams's story to suggest that there is any involvement of any sort with the Freemasons in the deaths of the five women on the streets of Whitechapel. However, it cannot be denied that one of the advantages of joining the Freemasons for a young man such as John Williams would be the innumerable contacts it would provide him with. Although there is no evidence for this, one thing that might have kept John Williams above suspicion later was that he did have contacts at the highest levels within the police force and the upper echelons of London society.

Of course, you cannot just join the Freemasons, you must be invited, and it is likely that the man who invited John Williams to join him in the brotherhood was his future father-in-law, Richard Hughes.

This was the time he'd met my great grandmother; it sounded like he was on the rebound. Being a man who always got what he wanted he must have been devastated to lose a woman to someone who was supposed to be a friend. Perhaps in the beginning Mary was someone who could take his mind off his emotional upset – did he know when he met her he was to marry someone else? As much as he might have thought of her, he knew he would marry someone more in his standing...sadly for Mary, who put her hopes of a better life in John's hands. My great grandmother must have believed the things he told her, why else would she up and leave her family to be with him? I wondered when the enchantment of a happy-ever-after wore off...if it ever did. Or was it the enigmatic doctor who decided enough was enough and finished the relationship? Whatever the reason, it would have been my great grandmother who lost out – emotionally and financially.

CHAPTER FIVE

Where they met we do not know, but, after the heartbreak over Annie Roberts, John was to turn his attention to a younger woman, Lizzie Hughes. The daughter of an industrialist, she lived in Morriston, Swansea. Morriston at the time was a thriving area of development and the Hughes family were highly thought of.

Richard Hughes was a partner in the Landore Tin Plate Works, established in 1851, and based in Swansea. He was one of four co-owners; the Landore was a large plant, one of the biggest and, in its day, one of the most modern in Wales. Later on, the site would also be used for one of the most revolutionary processes in steel making in the UK, but for the tin-plate manufacturers, times were good for the first forty years or so of their business. The company grew to employ almost one thousand people and was regarded as one of the more forward thinking parts of the industrialised belt in South Wales. When, in 1874, there was a massive strike throughout the region – caused by the employers locking out the workers who were seeking better rates of pay – it was the Landore workers who voted to return to work first, with the employers taking the opportunity to welcome them back by playing them into the pay office with a brass band. As they queued to collect their old rates of pay, the humiliation of the workers was complete.

In Lizzie Hughes, John Williams had chosen for himself a refined, talented, and religious girl. She played the organ in her local chapel and the congregation gave her a special present on her wedding day of a 'set of silver side dishes', together with a 'really beautiful Bible'. Quite what she expected from her husband is hard to know. Of course he needed her: a wife was 'almost a necessary part of a physician's professional equipment', said H. B. Thompson in *The Choice of a Profession*, published in 1857, because women would not feel comfortable being attended by a bachelor doctor. John Williams also thought this wife was more than a professional accoutrement and a social adornment; he believed that she would provide him with children.

Mary Elisabeth Ann Hughes was born in March

1850, the only daughter of Richard Hughes (born 1829) and Ann Thomas (born 1830). Richard Hughes's first wife died young, and he then married Mary, some 16 years his junior. Lizzie was obviously the apple of her father's eye, as we can see in the photos held in John Williams's archive at the National Library. An article about her marriage to John Williams, in April 1872, records that 'the bride herself' shows 'a willingness with which she has on occasions come forward to aid by her efforts and influence all movements having for the object the moral and religious improvement of the people…and the unassuming kindness of her disposition has endeared her to all her neighbours, who have watched her course from childhood upwards…'

This makes her sound a little saintly, but it is likely that, as an only daughter (and the only child born to a deceased wife) the mine-owner's daughter from parochial Wales was spoiled by her father. Marriage would be very different. Her husband, indeed society in general, would have strong opinions about how an eminent doctor's wife, in the centre of Victorian professional aristocracy, should behave. Whatever else we can sense about their marriage, despite signs of a closeness between the two of them at least in the initial stages, it was certainly a match that centred around him. The same newspaper report that gushed over Lizzie Hughes also tells us that the service was short, conducted in Welsh, and that he – not her, unlike in other marriage services of the time – was asked some questions. Lizzie's place in the marriage – silent and obedient – was firmly established from the outset.

Her diary for that year is one of the few objects belonging to her in the archive of the National Library, but it is he, not her, who fills in the first few entries. He records details of their wedding (but no mention is given to his beloved mother), spending about as much time recounting the amusing story of how his best man Marcus Beck slept through his connection on the train as he does on the wedding itself. As an afterthought, he adds: 'Liz looked in travelling dress better than ever'.

Both man and wife write entries during their honeymoon. Ever the worker, he spent a portion of their time on the continent visiting hospitals – one, Lizzie noted, 'appears more like a huge workhouse than an hospital' (23 April). Perhaps it was while on his honeymoon that John Williams forged contacts with other obstetricians that later led to him being an honorary member of a number of obstetrical societies all over the world.

In early May they returned home. Around the time that John Williams proposed to Lizzie, the opportunity to work in London had presented itself again. Lizzie went back to Wales while her husband, together with her father, travelled to London to sort out a suitable home for their married life. Lizzie retired to bed, writing (on 6 May) that she was 'in bed most of the day. Great fun watching the rabbits.' This immaturity raises doubts as to how she would have coped with the formidable society ladies in London; the naive girl from the provinces would have been overawed by the more worldly women she encountered through her husband's circle at UCH.

In her diary she continued to refer to her husband as Dr Williams. It was not until 21 June that she called him 'John' – which was interesting given that she referred to a number of her other friends by their first names.

It seemed that the marriage was one of convenience, or at least for John Williams. I felt quite sorry for his wife, it was obvious she felt intimidated by her new husband…it took several months before she felt she could call him by his first name. Even by Victorian standards it appeared to be odd behaviour…was he so authoritarian that she felt too nervous to question his authority?

He was evidently a powerful character with plenty of charisma…he had two women who had fallen for his charms…one whom he married but didn't really what to spend time with and the other whom he wanted to be with, but because of his social standing found it difficult to do so. To get ahead in London's society circle he needed his wife's money; or to be more precise, her father's.

Did Lizzie know about Mary? If she did, didn't it bother her?

I know I couldn't have turned a blind eye if I knew my husband was seeing another woman, but I also knew a lot of women did, probably like Lizzie Williams, in the hope that it would all dissipate. The fact that it happened at all would finish it for me.

I know I sound like I'm on my moral high horse but if you find yourself in a position where you want to be with someone else, you should tell your other half and either work it out with them or end the marriage. To carry on two relationships is surely going to end badly; as my great grandmother evidently found out.

One evening in late December 1871, a Welsh doctor called Fred Roberts was returning to London after performing an operation in Pembrokeshire. He stayed the night with a friend in Swansea, Dr Griffiths, and there he met one of Dr Griffiths's colleagues, Dr John Williams. They discussed a recent vacancy at University College Hospital, that of the position of Assistant Obstetric Physician. The position had not been filled and the two doctors urged John Williams to apply. Rather than write, John Williams travelled to London to apply for the post, but when he arrived the application period had closed and he was too late. However, the doctor saw the Dean, who decided that the young Welshman was an impressive candidate and so reopened the position, to which John Williams was successfully appointed. That which he had been after for some time – a return to the capital, and the chance to make his mark there – was back within his grasp.

Throughout John's career there was to be a question mark over the way that he was appointed to this position. On the surface, there was no impropriety, but this did not stop people considering it as somehow out of order. Even as late as 1891, an article appeared in which it was suggested that 'this was the beginning of the bitterness which has since dominated the intercourse between Dr Williams and a certain section of his colleagues'.

The questions this leaves begging are these: if he was so evidently the right candidate for the job – as shown by the Dean's decision to reopen the application process for him – why was he not considered before the advertisement was placed, or the process closed to applicants, by his former colleagues? Having worked in *exactly* that position only a few years previously, why was John Williams not considered straight away for the post?

He clearly did not have a champion at UCH, someone who wanted to see him appointed to the job, and one must assume that the person who stood in his way was his immediate superior, the Obstetric Physician, Dr Graily Hewitt. And was he truly ignorant of the job before being urged to apply for it by his two friends? Had he decided to settle down in Swansea until this opportunity was put in front of him? Something spurred his ambition – or had it just lain dormant for a while? Perhaps his marriage had reawakened it; perhaps his confidence had been dented by the move away from London, and it took the encouragement of friends to make him feel he was ready to move back there. Perhaps it was simply that he and his new bride wanted to experience life beyond Swansea, and the chance to do so arose at this most opportune of moments. What is certain is that his appointment provoked little admiration and a fair amount of envy.

Young doctors in those times did not expect this to be the way their careers began. In *The Medical Profession in Mid-Victorian London*, M. Jeanne Peterson writes:

'In his last year of medical studies, a student was required to serve at least three months as a clinical clerk to a hospital physician or as a dresser to a surgeon. These posts involved the basic care of medical and surgical patients in the wards under the supervision of the house physicians and surgeons, who were in turn responsible to the senior staff. Beyond the immediate educational value of these posts, they often had far-reaching career effects. Clerks or dressers serving under the same house-man became known as a "firm"'.

They often kept close ties, either personal or professional, long after medical school. Such friends could be a source of patients or consulting work. Senior men recommended their dressers and clerks to a variety of other appointments that helped them start their careers.

If he had ambitions to rise to 'the top of the tree' it was important to stay in London, to continue his affiliation with the world of hospitals and medical teaching, and eventually to gain appointments at the centre of English medical life.

Qualifying at the age of 21, the aspirant to consulting status stayed in London, serving in minor hospital posts, seeking the beginnings of practice, and making what connections and income he could. At age 26, he became a Fellow of his college and, with luck, by the age of 30 he might be appointed assistant physician or surgeon at one of the London hospitals.

In late July, they moved into 28 Harley Street, in the heart of London, and, shortly afterwards, 'John began doing Dr Hewitt's work'.

It was the custom for the hospital's doctors to contribute towards the costs of the hospital, since their hospital work enhanced their earning power in private practice. John Williams, the accounts show, paid the sum of three guineas as an annual subscriber. Interestingly, however, he was not the only Williams who was paying an annual subscription to the hospital. Next to his name was that of his brother, Morgan Williams, who made the rather more generous donation of £50 a year, and next to them both, listed as a Life Governor, 'by special appointment', was Mrs John Williams.

Here was the first notice of Lizzie Williams having a hand in her husband's day-to-day life. Why had she been granted this title? In 1886, she had worked on a fund-raising committee for the hospital's fancy-dress ball, staged that summer, which, together with a bazaar, made a profit of £3217: a fabulous sum, when you think that an annual salary for a nurse at that time was probably around £15. Mrs Williams had worked on the committee with Mrs Graily Hewitt, the wife of her husband's superior in the hospital. What was that relationship like? Mrs Williams came from Wales, so did Mrs Graily Hewitt patronise her as both a provincial girl and as the wife of the assistant to her husband? After this eventful summer, Mrs Williams made no further contribution to the records of the hospital's life, even though she remained a Life Governor.

If this was a template for a young doctor's career, then John Williams did not follow it. At almost every point, the young Welsh doctor did the opposite. So John Williams's return to London was very much against the grain. It must have been an interesting time for him to return – and to be set up with a house in Harley Street – when he was not a favourite with his seniors in the hospital. No wonder, then, that his first few years in London were financially tough for him. Did this help to set him apart further? Did the envy aroused because of the apparent ease of his appointment manifest itself in his peers obstructing his career in private practice? Was he always to be an outsider?

And being the outsider, did he feel that he had to work harder, to prove himself more, to discover something remarkable that no one else knew? To discover a cure or to refine a process that no one else had tried? A young doctor could make his name, his career, and his fortune this way. John Williams had been taught by one such man, Dr Joseph Lister. Was he inspired to do the same himself? After all, these were the times of innovation – of 'heroic' work by doctors. John Williams resolved to pioneer research on the uterus and the ovaries. Eager and ambitious, Dr Williams added to his workload under Dr Graily Hewitt by taking on the position of Medical Officer for Out-Patients at Queen Charlotte's Lying-In Hospital in Marylebone Road. With characteristic self-aggrandisement, he submitted his entry to the *Medical Directory* with the rather more pleasing title of Physician to the Out-Patients. Nothing available makes it clear what motivated John Williams to be an obstetrician, and to become the President of the Society of Obstetricians and Gynaecologists as part of his climb up the slippery slope of success, but it is certain that he was no sexual pervert. He was motivated, the evidence indicates, by a genuine desire to understand and conquer the diseases that fascinated him, *by whatever means at his disposal.*

Even the articles about his death revealed little about the research he undertook. Among the fullest entry in the *Lancet* was the obituary for John Williams, published on 5 June 1926.

The most revealing comment remains – that he found it hard to become established in private work, and that it was only thanks to his colleagues who helped to get him started that he took this route. This detail was recalled despite it being over fifty years since he had supposedly been struggling in private work. His difficulties, then, were of an order of magnitude that had not been fully appreciated.

But one of the most helpful books, partly because it confirms John Williams's absence from UCH around the time we believed him to be elsewhere, and partly because it yet again underlines the (at best) dismissive attitude of Victorian doctors to their subjects, was a catalogue that John Williams himself compiled.

One of the chief reasons why doctors were prepared to work at teaching hospitals such as UCH was because they were able to carry out research there. At UCH, a museum of 'specimens' illustrating their work aided this research, allowing students, as much as their teachers, to study. In 1891, John Williams, together with the Curator of the Museum, Charles Stonham, compiled a *Descriptive Catalogue of the Specimens Illustrating the Pathology of Gynaecology and Obstetrics Medicine Contained in the Museum of University College, London*. This catalogue runs to about seventy pages and is divided into seven sections:

Diseases of the Ovaries
Diseases of the Fallopian Tubes
Diseases of the Uterus
Diseases of the Vagina and External Organs of Generation
The Anatomy of Pregnancy
Injuries and Diseases incidental to Gestation and Parturition
Malformation of the Foetus

Entries within each section consist of a few lines of description, and are sometimes followed by an italicised passage outlining the patient's history and giving dates and places of removal of the exhibited part. Much of it makes for unpleasant reading. At first, John Williams's language seems quite cold, but it is soon apparent that it is simply observational; that is until he describes the 'papillomata covering the surface of the ovary' as 'a beautiful specimen'. The writer also appears devoid of compassion for the patient: when he describes a prolapsed uterus so inverted that 'it comes to lie outside the vulva', he records that 'the exposed part becomes, after a time, quite altered in character'. And painful, too, perhaps?

But Dr Williams's emotions were occasionally engaged. In a note about a woman who had been treated at UCH for eight years before her death, he writes: 'When dying, she requested that her body might be examined in order to satisfy her friends that she had been, during the early part of her disorder, the subject of unfounded suspicions and aspersions.' John Williams sees fit to record this in a document intended for his fellow physicians.

This was not just a catalogue for research: Dr Williams was also justifying, through his words, the work of anatomists. There were other smaller points to be drawn from this book. Some of the items in the museum were from private patients treated by John Williams; the 'uterus with sarcoma' of 4137a, for example. This woman, 38 years old, had been seeing John Williams for three years. Would a respectable private patient expect parts of her body to be on display in a university's museum? It was far more likely that this was a patient from the poorer part of town, a patient that Dr Williams saw while in Whitechapel. Her uterus would simply arrive at UCH in a jar in the doctor's hands, he would tell those who enquired that it came from a private patient – and no one would be any the wiser. He expands upon cases that he himself was involved with, such as the patient who had a cyst so large that 'two or three pailfuls of fluid were removed' from it (the patient died). But amongst these examples of John Williams performing 'heroic' surgical acts lie two crucial pieces of information. Items 4122 and 4091 were removed from two female patients on 31 August and 25 September 1888 respectively – but not by John Williams.

He dutifully records that they were removed by his assistant, Dr Herbert Spencer. The items removed were taken, *according to the notes made by John Williams*, from Emma Wood, who had her uterus and bladder removed; and Fanny Wright, who also had her uterus and bladder removed. Both women died. So where was Dr John Williams then and what was so important about those particular dates?

On 31 August, Mary Ann Nichols was killed. Both Liz Stride and Catherine Eddowes died on 30 September. John Williams, through the pages of the *Descriptive Catalogue*, had confirmed that he was not at UCH at the time of Mary Ann Nichols's death, and that he was also absent at around the time that Catherine Eddowes and Liz Stride were murdered.

He had also become a member of the Obstetrical Society of England and Wales. This excellent body would meet regularly to discuss papers presented by members, to air issues relating to their jobs (for example, the unregulated midwives that they sought to control), to examine unusual cases and dissect the malformed babies and other parts of the body that fellows around the country had encountered during their work. Their unquestioned superiority in Victorian society was evident at one meeting when an 18-year-old girl with anomalies to the skin around her nipples was brought in and asked to display her breasts to the forty or so fellows of the Society gathered in the room. There was no suggestion of a chaperone for her. The meeting continued with presentations from the doctors of the 'monsters', the deformed babies and deformed wombs that were offered up for fellows to volunteer to dissect.

Early on in his relationship with the society – within two years of joining – John Williams was made Honorary Secretary, yet, as ever, all was not plain sailing for him. It is interesting to read the proceedings of their meetings. There were usually between forty to fifty fellows present, sometimes more, with one or two distinguished visitors (often doctors from abroad), as well as a handful of doctors applying for membership. Often the papers presented were extraordinarily long and discussion of the paper would have to be postponed to the following meeting – John Williams himself was known for writing lengthily.

What is fascinating, though, is how contentious his papers seemed to be. The custom of the society was to thank the speaker for their paper before the floor was opened up for critical appreciation. In John Williams's case, fellows sometimes did not even bother with the polite remarks of thanks before launching into well-argued and reasoned attacks on his position on the issue of the moment. For example, after the Welsh doctor's presentation in May 1882 of a paper on 'The Natural History of Dysmenorrhoea', Dr Savage remarked that Dr Williams's paper was 'so long and elaborate that one forgot the beginning of it'. This treatment was not just meted out when he was a junior member of the society; even after he had been President in 1887, the other fellows were extraordinarily abrupt in their remarks.

From similar minutes in the college archives, we can see what John Williams's life at University College Hospital was like. He spent most of the 1870s consolidating his position there, and he expanded his repertoire by moving on from Queen Charlotte's and becoming a Consultant Physician at the Royal Infirmary for Women and Children at Waterloo. In 1880, he became Consultant Physician at the St Pancras and Northern Dispensary in the Euston Road. His private practice must have grown too, though not always easily; it would have helped this aspect of his career when he was made a Fellow of the Royal College of Physicians in 1879.

CHAPTER SIX

What kind of doctor was John Williams? The best source of material, at least in as much as he presented it, was in the *Transactions of the Obstetrical Society*, the official record of the Society of Obstetricians and Gynaecologists, of which he was a prominent member – indeed, later on, its president. The minutes in the *Transactions* were fascinating. It was obvious that he was highly thought of by his colleagues; and yet those who disagreed with him were numerous, and they made their objections known. Was this because of simple snobbery? Was he looked down upon because he was Welsh? Or was it because of something else? Were they envious of his successes?

Going through the volumes of the *Transactions* from 1875, when John Williams was elected to the council of the society, up to the time he was president, it was clear that there were certain protocols that had to be followed. Each season began with the President's address: he would outline aspects of the profession and its development that he felt most deserved notice, and usually take the opportunity to draw attention to his own research. Thereafter, he would be expected to make the first reply to the papers delivered to the society by one of its fellows, and often to sum up the argument at the end of the discussion that followed. Finally, he would direct his fellows as to who should dissect the deformed foetuses and other materials presented to the society which formed part of their discussions.

However, John Williams was never as popular a fellow or president as others around him – Dr Francis Champneys, for instance, who was clearly well liked and is accorded respect in books about obstetrics even today. John Williams, on the other hand, was scorned by some of his colleagues and, when he took issue with the proposition put forward in Dr Dakin's 'Sarcometous Uterus removed by Vaginal Hysterectomy' paper in April 1890, was shouted down by all the fellows present – Dr Macnaughton-Jones called John Williams's views 'fallacious'.

No other president of the society seemed to be criticised in the way that John Williams was – yet he seemed to thrive on these attacks, as if they confirmed for him that he was right.

Much of the criticism was probably unfair, as it came from those who were reluctant to put into practice the kind of protocols that had become standard then, such as the practice of 'Listerism' which John Williams, along with Dr Champneys, championed. The fuddy-duddies within the profession were determined to resist these new-fangled ways, and looked all the more foolish for it. Perhaps it is wrong to see these attacks in *such* simple terms; but elsewhere the same sort of reaction to him as a colleague was evident. In the archive of UCH, the minutes of the meeting in 1893, at which John Williams's retirement from active duty at the hospital was also announced, record his appointment as a consultant. No letter of resignation from him was read out, as was customary, and, more importantly, no vote of thanks for his work was taken.

Among the items in John Williams's archive in the National Library in Aberystwyth was a copy of an article dated 15 August 1891 from a magazine called the *Gentlewoman*. This is fascinating because it provides an opinion of John Williams as a practitioner, from an independent source. The article was part of a series, entitled 'Medicos under the Microscope', and many doctors before Williams had come under the author's scrutiny. The article provides insights that are not found in any other source, but the context is not clear. It was important to consult other copies of the magazine; not only for what it said about Williams, but also at the magazine itself – was this piece in keeping with the rest of the magazine? And were the opinions expressed here about Williams similar to those about others?

The *Gentlewoman* can be read at the British Library's newspaper archive at Colindale, a grim-looking building in north London. The library is an extraordinary mine of material, and real, not microfilmed, copies of the paper are a joy to look at. All the original advertisements, everything from soap to stays, nestle alongside the instructive and patronising text. Articles on the law (by 'Portia') and on the city (by 'Cassandra'), sit alongside more gossipy pieces such as 'Cosy Corner Chat' which fills two or three pages with nonsense such as:

'Just fancy this! There are between 36,000,000 and 37,000,000 born in the world every year, that is at the rate of about 70 per minute, more than one for every beat of the clock. Poor little things!'

Skipping past 'Famous People I Have Met', the tone of some of the magazine is summed up by a heading 'French Books That May Be Read'. This however, was at odds with some of the regular articles – those on the city and on the law – which set out to be useful rather than simply judgemental. This was obviously the aim of 'Medicos under the Microscope': 'next week', the magazine announced in January 1891, 'will appear the first of a series of articles under the above heading, a list that comprises the Galahads of the profession'. The series would cover general practitioners, surgeons, specialists and obstetricians.

The anonymous author – who signed herself, in Greek, 'Microscopist' – pointed to existing rules, which forbade doctors from advertising. This, she felt, justified the publication of such a series of quick portraits, as it gave their readers both an idea of what was felt about other doctors in London and elsewhere, and an insight into how their own doctor was seen. The articles were written, the subheading continued, 'with a full knowledge of the Laws, written and unwritten, which forbid Doctors to adopt any of the ordinary forms of publicity'. The writer goes on to say, 'the Medical Men included in this series have not been invited to sit for their pen portraits. But the pictures will not be any the less true to life because their subjects have no hand in their preparation, nor even knowledge of their production.'

Unsurprisingly perhaps, the series attracted a great deal of criticism from the medical press, though having read all the articles in the series it is hard to see why. Almost all of them are flattering, with one or two exceptions: William Playfair, in the 1 August 1891 issue, and John Williams, in the 15 August 1891 issue, are the only two doctors who merit anything negative from 'Microscopist'.

The article about John Williams is worth quoting in full as it tells us a lot about Dr Williams that we have no other source for. Apart from being an independent point of view, it is, perhaps more importantly, a woman's point of view – when almost all the other tributes and recollections we have of him are from men. Although, of course, Queen Victoria's tributes to him are fulsome, he was surely on his best behaviour with her.

'Microscopist' and others like her saw a different side to the doctor. A highly revealing note scribbled by Williams on the top of the article says, 'I should like to have met Microscopist. She must have been a little girl I think.'

Dr John Williams is a very difficult man with whom to deal. He presents a combination of qualities so unusual that it requires greater space than I have at my command to do him justice.

There is no use in attempting to disguise the fact that here exists a prejudice against Dr Williams. It is intangible perhaps, hard to analyse, but, like hydra-headed scandal, it is equally hard to kill. It is best to grapple with it boldly, drag it to light, and see what effect free ventilation will have upon it.

John Williams commenced his professional life as

a general practitioner at Swansea. From this somewhat lowly position he was suddenly, and to the surprise of London medical circles, appointed to a vacancy on the staff of King's College Hospital. Envious colleagues whispered of 'wire-pulling'; those who, apparently, were well informed were prepared with details. It remained to Sir William Jenner to explain, and Sir William Jenner did not explain. This was the beginning of the bitterness which has since dominated the intercourse between Dr Williams and a certain section of his colleagues. More was to follow, equally vague, equally indefinite. He was created *Accoucheur* to HRH Princess Beatrice. Why?

The envious ones could not understand it; they cannot understand it now, and the fact that Sir John Williams's name is so frequently before the public has but increased their chagrin. It has also increased his practice. There are people so curiously constituted that it gives them a real pleasure to be associated with Royalty, even in the distant and slender way of having the same medical attendant. It is perhaps true that Dr Williams has profited by the snobbishness of the British public, but is he to be held responsible for this?

I am no blind partisan of Dr Williams. I admit that he has not established by any valuable book, new discovery of brilliant cure, a claim to be considered as the leading London obstetrician. But for all that I am prepared to assert that he is an able man, resourceful and practical, level-headed in an emergency, cool and wide awake. Her Royal Highness knew what she was about. If he will never set the Thames on fire, he will at least never admit his abortive attempts to compass that conflagration. His reticence is a valuable quality; that he relaxes it a little when on the subject of his position and influence is, to my way of thinking, the only regrettable feature in his character.

He has been conspicuously successful with the public; he is making a large income; other men are not. This is the *crux* of the whole thing, and 'it is a jealous people'.

I admit there are men who are equally successful who are not equally unpopular. But Dr Williams has not the *suaviterin modo*. If he wants to say that he does not care to undertake gynaecological operations, he is not content with a modest hint on the subject. A graceful retirement from a portion of his practice, never onerous, is not the course he pursues. He asserts himself aggressively. He issues a letter, a sort of royal proclamation, and to enforce its importance he signs it conjointly with Dr Champneys. But when so much is admitted, it must be confessed it was a very venial crime, not deserving of the burst of indignation that followed. From another man it would have been laughed at and forgotten. That he models himself upon the traditions of Dr Matthews Duncan, that he is a Jesuit, that he is blatantly vain and inordinately dogmatic, are assertions that may beat once dismissed. The old adage of the chain and its weakest link suffices for them all. Dr John Williams, far from being a Jesuit, is a Welsh Methodist, almost its exact antithesis!

So much for the demon Rumour.

The simply furnished reception room at 63 Brook Street is usually full of ladies who cast surreptitiously inquiring glances at each other, and seem to be engaged in a species of mild mental arithmetic. A husky parrot with a distressing cough relieves the monotony of waiting and endeavours feebly to say a few words. But ornothologically considered, it is not to be mentioned in the same way with the bird of like species possessed by Dr David Ferrier [who owns a 'lively, beautiful' parrot who calls out that it is 'poorly' all the time].

When the patient reaches the consulting-room, after a dignified wait, she finds herself in a light and cheerful room – commodious, staid, and simple. Sometimes Dr Williams rises with benignant courtesy, but sometimes his brow is overladen with care, and he is studiously abrupt. These are the times when, so to speak, dynasties are in his hands, and common mortals sink into insignificance. He is handsome, prosperous, portly, on first impression. Later, one discovers that he is not quite handsome; his lips are a thought too full, his eyes are too weakly blue. Not quite prosperous – or why those tell-tale lines? Not quite portly – the ample proportions are more promise than performance. He is not quite convincing, he is not quite impressive, but he is very near both those standards. His hair is grey, his close trimmed whiskers grey also. His hands are white and well cared for, he dresses well, his voice, though a little hard sometimes, is pleasant. All the time one talks to him, one wonders, 'why don't they like him?' And there is no answer, or if there be one, it is not known to *'Microscopist'*

CHAPTER SEVEN

In 1881, John Williams has left us a diary of his trip to the West Indies, and it affords us a rare insight into the state of his marriage. His handwriting is difficult to decipher, almost impossible in the later pages. The writing starts off clean and fine but swiftly becomes crabbed and slanted. The transcripts supplied by the Library omit the more unreadable passages. But, as one of the few records that allows us to see something of their married life and how distant he seemed from her, it is invaluable. The diary has only survived in a partial form, so we do not get to read about everything they experienced on their trip.

Nevertheless, we can make out enough to get a sense of their voyage and what they experienced. They visited Jamaica and Barbados, and neither of them was a particularly good sailor. Once on dry land, John Williams seems to spend most of his time away from his wife, out riding in the hills with his new travelling companions. This extract from his diary gives a rare insight into their relationship.

Everything having been made ready, we started from Waterloo station by Royal Mail carriages to Southampton, where we paid dock dues (6/-) and were put on board the tender which took us on board the 'Para' which was lying out in Southampton water. We soon found our cabin (150/4) which was a very nice room in the fore part of the ship, with two berths and a sofa. Into this we had our luggage carried & we took out things we immediately required & went on the Quarterdeck to see what was going on. There were a jolly number of people – many of whom were friends of passengers coming to see them off. The most-troubled was a little boy about 12 years of age who saw his Mother off, he was crying bitterly. About 3.30 the bell rang & all for shore went on the tender – & after they had cheered us lustily we parted – they for England & we for the West Indies.

We got on board the Para soon after 12 o'clock – but we were delayed by the arrival of the mails &

we did not sail until 5 minutes before four. We went briskly along – but the weather was a little hazy – to see the coast of the Isle of Wight cliffs. We sat down to dinner about 5.30 & enjoyed it. Went to bed early about 8 o'clock, I slept well.

Sunday Sept 18th

Got up about 8 o'clock & felt rather qualmish. Lizzie had some tea & was sick after it. I drank none & was sick without. But we had not much sickness all day Sunday. We were on deck most of the time but we took no food whatsoever. Went to bed about quarter past 7. It was rather squally in the night and & the ship rolled a little.

Monday Sept 19th

Very qualmish – much sickness. Went on deck & remained there the greatest part of the time until about 5.30. Then went to bed. Got more squally towards night & the rolling of the ship was worse. I took no food all day.

Tuesday Sept 20th

Felt ill, remained in bed. Living on ice & iced water and lemonade. Ice was by far the best stuff for it. When I had plenty of ice it felt quite comfortable. Lizzie remained in bed Tuesday, Wednesday altogether but was up for a part of the day on Thursday. Had some hot beef tea.

Wednesday Sept 21st
At last – was much better though with no food.

Thursday Sept 22nd
Got up early. Had 3 eggs for breakfast and some iced water and bread – Lizzie in bed but with some food. I dined and lunched in the saloon. Had hot bath.

Friday Sept 23rd
Had a sea and shower bath. Glowing. Sea has been smooth since yesterday, no rolling. Delightful weather. Warm breeze on deck, no rain. We had very heavy rain on Tuesday & Wednesday. Very hungry.

Lizzie lunched in the saloon today. Has been on deck all day. I never had a better night's sleep than last night. Lizzie did not feel so well in the evening, did not go into dinner. I ate a very hearty dinner.

Lizzie went to bed early – I went about 9.30. Hot night. The weather is getting hot – but there is a beautiful breeze on deck and amid ships where the hatches are open.

Saturday Sept 24th

Got up early and had a bath – but felt qualmish all day. Went in to breakfast and lunch though but not to dinner. Lizzie has been qualmish all day and sick several times. Had some hot soup made for Lizzie, & she was better towards night. Went to bed early 6.30, slept through the best part of the night. Lizzie had a pretty good night.

Sunday Sept 25th

Got up early & had a bath and went up walking on the quarter deck for several hours before breakfast. Lizzie much better. Has taken a good deal of beef jelly, looks better, less qualmish & no sickness. I went & had breakfast & then church at 10.30, where the archdeacon read the Litany and preached a short sermon. Went to lunch and then there was some hymn singing in the afternoon. There was some singing again in the evening. Went to bed early.

Sunday Oct 2nd

We had service in the morning, read by the captain. It was a very hot day one of the hottest we have had. Very fine, and the sea as smooth as a lake. Lizzie spent the great part of the day on deck – but in the afternoon she went down to the saloon, as it was cooler there.

The diary then skips several days and we learn that the ship has landed safely in Jamaica. It is noticeable how little he writes about Lizzie now that he can no longer play doctor to her.

Thursday Oct 27th

Started with Mr D at 9.30 to see the shrine in the Valley. Went on a pretty ride along the slopes and on the leeward side – passed through several negro villages – little huts –until we got to the valley. There Mr D had to marry a nice couple. A boy went with me and showed me Mr Edward Phillips' house – a preacher, a Blackman about 45 years of age, he gave me a drink of coconut which was very good. He rode with me to the shrine which is situated about a mile up the valley, close to the beacon. It is a very large purple red structure with an inclined face towards the river. The highest part of this shrine is about 8 feet high. We afterwards called on Mr H – the manager of the Rutland Estate – then returned to wish Mr Philips goodbye and rode to meet Mr L – met him on the ridge and then rode to Kingston together – which we reached at 3.30. Mr Hazell – Mr and Mrs Hughes & Mr Brauch dined at Mr L's this evening. Mr Brauch's son wants to become a doctor & Mr Hazell's son is going to be a Barrister.

Friday Oct 28th

Rode with Mr Mc L to see the spa and drink the water. It is a powerful opening in the S Valley – built around with bricks. I was told it was chalky water but I found it was nothing of the sort. The water is like London water and very nice. We sailed about 7 in the evening, got to Barbados about 6in the morning – after a very smooth journey.

The diary entries are sparse and repetitive for a few days, with more details of seasickness and occasional meals, before John Williams is able to say he is better once more.

Sunday Nov 6th

My birthday. Lizzie is still qualmish. Sunday night at 9 o'clock was beautiful – and we went to bed thinking we were going to get beautiful weather.

Monday Nov 7th

Wind and sea more about 4 inches this evening – and it blew a severe gale all day and Monday night. The stern of the vessel dipped under the waves.

Tuesday Nov 8th

Wakening at 9 o'clock with wind and sea subsided and we had a beautiful day.

Wednesday Nov 9th
Beautiful day. Both well.

Thursday Nov 10th
Lizzie for first time at breakfast. Beautiful day.

The writing in these extracts does not suggest a passionate marriage. Was he trying to make amends for his shortcomings as a husband? Was he trying to forget about my great grandmother? Perhaps he thought that Lizzie would fall pregnant. Whatever his reasons for taking a cruise it seems he failed to inject any romance into his marriage. Quite the contrary, it seemed that he might as well have been travelling alone, for all the enjoyment went to him. Lizzie it seems didn't see anything of the West Indies or meet any of the inhabitants that John had written about. Was she just there for proliferation purposes? There didn't seem there was much love lost between them and I wondered if he showed my great grandmother any emotional attachment because it was quite obviously missing from his marriage.

He was more committed to his work than his marriage and that part of his life went from strength to strength.

One picture of his private career was provided by some letters sent by John Williams in his capacity as doctor, held in the archive of the Asquith family kept in the Bodleian Library in Oxford. Margot Asquith – who wrote in her autobiography that she had visited factory girls in Whitechapel in 1888 – became a patient of John Williams in the 1890s. These letters give a rare glimpse of what it was like for a private patient to have him as a doctor, and the tone of some of the letters that he wrote to her over the years is surprising. He continued to write to her until after the First World War, and his last letter gives details of the visit paid to the National Library by some of her stepchildren, including Lady Bonham Carter.

Margot's first pregnancy, which resulted in a stillbirth, was a very difficult one and 'it was entirely owing to his [John Williams's] skill that she survived at all,' says Colin Clifford in his biography of the Asquiths published in 2002. The doctor told her to rest in bed for six weeks, after which she left London to return to her home at Glen in Scotland. In the letter that he then wrote to her some weeks later, John Williams appears more like a lover than a doctor. The strength of emotion is undeniable for someone who, up until now, had appeared a fairly dry and distant person – particularly so given that he had recently delivered the woman of a dead child.

Once again, we puzzled our way through his handwriting, but had to concede defeat with some words. The 'little children' he refers to are her stepchildren, from Herbert Asquith's first marriage.

31 July 1895
Dear Child,

I trust the journey north did not over-fatigue you and that you reached Glen none the worse for it. Your advent there must have been hailed with pleasure by everyone, especially by the little children who must have been delighted to have their Margot with them again. The period of convalescence after an illness in this dismal place can never be anything but depressing, and you must have found it very much so since its frequent [maddening?] drawback. I wish you could have bounded into health at once – but at Glen you will find it very difficult. You will recover strength by leaps and bounds and the air of Scotland will soon bring back the roses to your pale cheeks.

Do not think – do not brood at any rate – over the past – but look to what is to come, and that with a brave and cheerful heart. Brave you have been, and more I know you will be, and a time will come when you will be amply rewarded. I cannot tell you how much I feel indebted to you for all your patience, [?], faith, goodness and trustfulness.

A sense of pleasure will always prevail over all

others whenever I shall look back upon the time during which I have known you – a time (forgetful and negligent as I am) which cannot pass out of my memory. You have given me a new pleasure in life, and in watching you and your husband (and I shall watch you) and the part you play in moulding the future of the country. I shall have a new and [?] interest. You gave me this.

I hope you found Sir Charles well, please to convey to him expressions of my high esteem, tell your husband that I shall expect to see your real self in October and believe that I am devoted to you [?], J. W.

The letter that follows in the collection is all the more remarkable because of what precedes it. Written some five years later, John Williams is still in Brook Street, but his humour is worse; and although he is evidently still good friends with Margot Asquith, the warmth of his earlier communication is missing. The tone – from the way he addresses her, through to the way he signs off the letter – is radically different from that of the earlier letter.

25 Nov 1900

Dear Mrs Asquith,

I do not know, nor have I any wish to know, indeed I would rather not know, what my [inquisitor?] told you of my wife, but I gather that it was something the reverse of complimentary.

Fortunately I am almost if not quite indifferent as to the opinions of most people about me and mine – and on this point I think that I am quite indifferent. There are two things that are always welcome to me: opposition to abuse: anything that is offensive – praise which produces [largesse?] and general [vileness?]: one thing that at our time would have been intolerable, crushing neglect. I cannot complain of the last. Here ends all thought of your letter.

Oddly I have during the last fortnight been troubled beyond measure by the foolish and wicked talk of so called friends respecting a friend of mine now dead. I have had to speak and write much with a view to try and stop the tongues of scandal which under the circumstances should have been absolutely silent. Success however was very partial, and the words of the sturdy old thinker 'the poison of an asp is other than lawful [?]' have often occurred to me as often [?] as the modern rendering [?] 'Speak no slander, nor listen to it.' The morbid state of mind which is so common is I believe greatly on the increase and this increase is largely due to the penny press. O for a heavy box of paper.

Many thanks for Napoleon. I shall read it with pleasure at least for the sake of the sender [?] as I had it not. Nor did I intend to obtain it, because I was not favourably impressed by the notices of it I had seen in the papers. Nor has Napoleonology [?] been a favourite study with me.

Yours always very truly

John Williams

What had been said about Lizzie? Who had said it? On what grounds? Was this the confirmation that we had been looking for all along, that there was something wrong in his marriage about which we were never going to know more? Who was this friend whom he felt he had to defend? Could it be anyone we've already read about? Against what sort of attacks? The slander that should have been 'silent' – was this something he was only too well aware of himself? Unfortunately, this is a mystery that cannot be solved – no other letters in the collection remain that could clarify the identity of the person any further. None of the later letters returns to this theme. They are either pleas for her to visit him in Aberystwyth, or letters encouraging her husband – by then the prime minister – to greater things. One letter, dated 26 August 1912, refers to 'little Anthony' (who grew up to be a successful film director) and recalls something of his own childhood:

'John Williams enjoyed the high society. The *Lancet* of 17 March 1888 carried the following announcement: 'HRH Princess Beatrice, Princess Henry of Battenburg, has been pleased to appoint John Williams, MD, to be physician *accoucheur* to Her Royal Highness.'

Princess Beatrice was married to Prince Henry of Battenburg, and, before John Williams was appointed to be her physician *accoucheur*, they had had two children together. The two eldest were Alexander, born on 23 November 1886, and Victoria Eugenie, born on 24 October 1887, who went on to become Queen of Spain and died in 1969. John Williams was in attendance at the birth of Leopold (born in 1889; he died before John Williams, in 1922), and Maurice, born in 1891, who also died young, in 1914.

Princess Beatrice was Queen Victoria's youngest daughter and was known as 'Baby' to her mother. Like Victoria, Beatrice suffered the early death of her husband and, having spent most of her youth at her mother's side, went on to spend a large part of her adult life with her as well. She was entrusted by Victoria with the task of compiling and preparing for publication the Queen's journals and letters, and naturally she removed passages she felt posterity need not know about. Luckily for historians, however, the Queen and Prince Albert had foreseen this, and had privately printed some material already – so giving us insights into Victoria's feelings on her wedding night, for instance.

But 'Baby' did something else for her mother. She introduced her to John Williams, and in the last years of the Queen's life the Welsh doctor was to become a support for her and her family.

John Williams had already proved his worth to the royal family not only with Princess Beatrice, but also with her brother's daughter-in-law, the Duchess of York (and later Queen Mary), whom he first attended in 1894.

For the boy from the valleys that moment must have been one of the greatest in his life. Not only had he helped at the birth of children who would one day become kings, but he was now in a position to command the highest fees for his private work. He had secured the best possible endorsement for his services. Other members of the wider royal family wrote to Queen Victoria to thank her for recommending Dr John Williams to them. No doubt he went to visit them when they required his services – no chance of royalty, however minor, having to sit patiently in his Mayfair waiting room – and his stock would have increased enormously around London as a result.

Interestingly, another element of Williams's private life can be glimpsed through these papers. In his journals, the Duke of York would paste in the occasional newspaper clipping, and one such (in 1894) gives details of the christening of the young Prince Edward (known in the family by one of his other names, David, and later titled, after his abdication, the Duke of Windsor). In the list of those attending the christening is John Williams, but not Mrs Williams. In all the times that the doctor stayed close to the royal family, he never seemed to have taken his wife with him. It is understandable that they would not invite her when he was there to help with the birth of a child, but given the personal reaction of the Duke of York, and the fact that the christening John Williams attended was only in south-west London, in Sheen, not very far from his home, it seems odd that his wife did not go with him.

John Williams's archive in the National Library of Wales also contains telegrams, letters and other materials sent by the Queen, and some members of her family, and these can be compared with the information learned from the archives at Windsor. There were two telegrams from Queen Victoria, addressed to him at Sandringham, oddly insistent about asking him to write and telegram her. The first was clear: this must have come to him at the time of the birth of Albert, later to be King George VI, and her message – 'Please telegraph again tonight and twice for the next 2 days – daily till the 10th day and write please daily till then' – was simply because she was so concerned about the Duchess of York and about her new baby.

In the royal archives, there are copies of John Williams's replies: 18 December, 12.19 p.m.; 19 December, 10.10 a.m.; 20 December 10.17 a.m.; 21 December, 10.21 a.m.; 22 December, 1.05 p.m.; and 23 December, 11.40 a.m. They all say roughly the same thing – mother and baby doing fine.

What makes less sense is the telegram that Queen Victoria sent from Balmoral to John Williams in London in October 1895 – 'Hope you will write to me again.' It is a little plaintive in tone, even pathetic. What is extraordinary is that no birth is happening or even due at that time, and therefore it would seem that the Queen is asking him to write to her not with news of grandchildren and great-grandchildren, but simply for the pleasure of hearing from him. So it seemed, until we found that he continued to correspond with other members of the family, especially those whose births he had attended. John Williams had presided at the birth of five of the children of Prince George, the Duke of York. His wife Mary, who was the Duchess of Teck before becoming Duchess of York, was formerly his brother Eddy's fiancée, before Eddy died. Incidentally, Eddy was the royal 'suspect' as far as many Ripperologists were concerned.

Edward David, the eldest, would grow up to fall in love with Mrs Simpson, an American divorcée, and abdicate before he was crowned king. Albert George, the first child delivered by John Williams, named after his great-grandfather, would grow up to take the place of his brother, albeit reluctantly, and become king through the Second World War, before the crown passed on to his daughter Elizabeth. The Princess Royal, the Duchess of Harewood, worked as a nurse at the children's hospital in Great Ormond Street for two years. Henry would become the Duke of Gloucester and Governor General of Australia, and his brother George was rumoured to have become a drug addict and had affairs with Noel Coward, among others. He became the Duke of Kent, before dying in a plane crash in 1942. The youngest son, John, was born on 11 July 1905, like almost all his brothers and sisters except for the eldest, at York Cottage in Sandringham. His delivery took place some years after John Williams had retired from private practice, and over a decade after he had stopped working in the public hospitals, so long after he had given up practising medicine. Indeed, John Williams had abandoned living in London altogether and would have had to travel to Sandringham from Wales, in order to attend the birth of a royal baby one last time. The boy born that night was not considered well and, by his fourth birthday, was diagnosed as suffering from a severe kind of epilepsy. This had a profound effect on his development and he was removed from the rest of his family (who were allegedly disturbed by his fits) and lived apart from them for most of the rest of his short life. Today he is remembered as 'the lost prince'.

John Williams was to remain in contact with the boy that he had delivered until he died; in the archive of the National Library of Wales is a letter sent to John Williams, only one year before Prince John died, thanking him for the gift of a book. (John Williams sent all the children of the Duke and Duchess of York – the 'Georgie pets', as their grandparents, Edward VII and his wife, called them – Christmas presents all through their youth. They would dutifully thank him and send him Christmas cards by way of return.) The letter is from one of the Queen's ladies-in-waiting, and in it she thanks John Williams for the 'charming book' which he had sent to the Prince, and which 'has much pleased him'. Although the Prince's thanks do not come directly – Charlotte Bell, known as Lalla, the Prince's constant companion, passes them on – there is a poignant note added to the letter: 'The Queen wishes me also to thank you for your kind thought for the poor dear boy.'

Prince John died in Sandringham in 1919. Contrary to the impression received by many people, he did not spend his life hidden entirely from public view, merely the last few years of it, and there are photographs of him in John Williams's archive.

There are even Christmas cards that bear his name, addressed to the doctor and signed by all the young princes and the princess.

Prince John's signature is traced in black ink over pencil marks, and drawn between two pencil lines to show him where to finish the loops and curves of his writing. In other words just what you would expect from a small child learning to write, but not from one already in his early teens.

Someone who was so familiar with the Queen, on such easy terms with her and her family, would have appeared above suspicion to those he associated with in Whitechapel and elsewhere.

He had, after all, been chosen from among many to be the doctor to the Queen's beloved youngest child before the murders took place, news that would have been widely circulated in the world in which he moved.

John Williams had already proved his worth to the royal family not only with Princess Beatrice, but also with her brother's daughter-in-law, the Duchess of York (and later Queen Mary), whom he first attended in 1894.

It was immediately clear that the royal family held John Williams in high esteem, and that he played his role as the attentive family doctor very well. Queen Victoria wrote about him being 'very quiet' and 'gentle and kind'.

CHAPTER EIGHT

The best record of a doctor's career, and the institutions in which he worked during that time, is in *The Medical Directory*. *The Medical Directory* is a fascinating and invaluable volume, recording particulars of registered doctors, and the institutions throughout the British Isles where they worked. These included both privately- and publicly-run institutions. Alongside the institutional entries, each doctor submitted an entry that gave their qualifications, their employment history and, if they wished, a list of their publications. There in black and white was John Williams's name, his address, where he had studied, which hospitals and other medical establishments he worked for, which societies he belonged to, and the papers he had written for various learned journals.

However, there was no mention anywhere in the brief notes he made for the 1900 edition of the volume that Dr Williams had worked in Whitechapel. The entry listed Sir John's places of work as:

Royal Hospital for Women and Children
University College Hospital
St Pancras and Northern Dispensary
General Lying-In Hospital

It was apparent that John Williams, if nothing else, was a workaholic, for in addition to all this he also must have had a private practice. How could he possibly have found time on top of his other commitments to run a clinic in Whitechapel as well?

John Williams embarked on 1888 in a mixed state of mind; work was all consuming for him, he seemed to fill every waking hour with appointments, meetings, visits, operations. The Society of Obstetricians expressed its gratitude to him for putting his 'valuable time' at its disposal, thus suggesting that he used every moment of the day to work. Add to this the pressure that even a seemingly harmless court case can bring – especially to one who values public opinion so highly, and not just for reasons to do with his work – and we can begin to appreciate the mental state he was in.

After the autumn of 1888, and over the next few years, John Williams cut himself adrift from the past, a little bit at a time. He requested that he be allowed to stop performing 'ovariotomies', and he stood down from various committees at UCH.

In 1893, he retired altogether from the active staff at UCH, citing ill-health as one of the reasons, though he lived for a further 53 years. He was made Consultant Obstetric Physician of the hospital, and in 1894 received royal recognition of his role, when he was created a baronet. He adopted the motto *bydd gyfiawn ac nac ofna*, which translates as 'Be just and fear not'. Sir John Williams and his wife Lizzie moved into Sir William Jenner's old home in 63 Brook Street in 1896, and this became his private surgery as well.

Closer to home, a private matter was preoccupying John Williams. His wife, it would seem, was unable to have children. Given his arrogance, it is safe to assume that he never for one moment thought that the failure of the marriage to produce children might have been because of him. Instead we can observe, from outside the marriage, the changes this disappointment wrought upon Lizzie. From being the plump, cheery-looking girl seen in her youthful photograph, she became thin, browbeaten, and altogether a shadow of her former self. Her husband's intense interest in genealogy was underpinned by a more personal determination to replace his dead older brother David, and ensure that the Williams family line continued. His brother Morgan remained unmarried, and Nathaniel, who married the year after John, was never to have children, in contrast to the other side of the family who seemed to produce cousins in large numbers.

Lizzie Hughes had a sad life. Her mother died when she was young and she married a man older than her, who, all the evidence suggests, did not really cherish her as much as she might have wished. Even after their trip, which was maybe meant to be a 'second honeymoon', she failed to produce the children they both craved. For some reason – be it this mutual disappointment, or maybe she was suffering from some illness – her husband never fully integrated her into his life. It was interesting to learn that she did not attend important events with him.

He had persuaded her to marry him – presumably her father, impressed by his future son-in-law, helped press his case – but there appears more of a sense of duty in the marriage than love.

If some illness prevented her from having children, maybe the depression that ensued drove them further apart. Maybe a sense of marital duty was enough for Lizzie, but it was clearly not enough for her husband.

We know from his records that John was obsessed by

John Williams and his wife
Lizzie, photographed in the
late 1880s.

Mary Kelly's granddaughter, who told the story of her grandmother's shocking death.

Above: John Williams's knife, which fits the description of the knife used on the Ripper's victims.

Below: The grave of Mary Ann Nichols, the Ripper's first victim.

The graves of Catherine Eddowes and Mary Kelly, the fourth and fifth victims.

genealogy. He put a tremendous amount of work not only into his own lineage but also his wife's, as if he was tracing the absence of issue through the bloodline. It is reasonable to assume, from the intensity of his relationship with his mother (matched only by that of Nathaniel's), that he wanted to see everything she had achieved continued through the generations. A remark by Ruth Evans, his biographer, confirms his unhappiness: 'the one great sadness of his life was that he had no children'.

Did he regret not marrying my great grandmother? She could have borne him children. She loved him enough to leave her husband and children, and for what? He didn't love his wife, yet he had no intention to leave her either. Did my great grandmother realise this after a time…would she live to regret it? Or face something worse?

Dr Ilott, whom he had met one evening at the Society of Obstetricians and Gynaecologists, introduced John Williams to the Infirmary. Dr Ilott had joined the society in the year that John Williams became Honorary Secretary of the society; there is no doubt the two men would have known each other in those circumstances. Both doctors, after all, would have joined the society for the same reason – advancement. This was an opportunity to meet like-minded men, discuss their working conditions, hear papers presented on the new kinds of treatment being practised in the capital, and occasionally welcome visitors from further afield or even abroad to discuss their work with them. Dr Ilott would have been particularly keen to associate with his fellow doctors; a medical man within the workhouse infirmaries did not expect his work to increase his prestige, rather the reverse. Perhaps when they first talked, Dr Ilott simply invited Dr Williams to come and visit, to see the condition of the women in his care, and asked for the benefit of his wisdom; perhaps he had a specific case in mind to discuss with the doctor. At some point, though, in the course of the weeks following their first meeting, John Williams took a carriage east to Whitechapel, and walked through the workhouse gates for the first time.

Was he risking much as a junior doctor in doing so? We can presume that he had begun to find his feet in terms of his work in private practice; the fact that he had enough surplus money to start buying up the books and manuscripts that were later to be housed in the National Library in Aberystwyth indicates this.

We can guess that life under Dr Graily Hewitt at University College Hospital was still tricky, judging from the irascible way the doctor took issue with John Williams's papers at the society's meetings; and perhaps that meant that the research the young Welshman needed to carry out, in order to achieve the kind of breakthrough that would earn him his reputation, was hampered by the control exerted over him by Dr Graily Hewitt. So a trip to the East End, to visit pliant and willing patients, would have been welcome indeed.

Whitechapel was a place of fascination to many Victorians, many of whom were painfully aware of the extent of the poverty there, and, acting upon their religious and social convictions, tried to do something about it. For many others, it was a place where they could show the extent of their philanthropy, and visit the area to 'do good works', before returning to their comfortable homes in the sure knowledge they had just improved their chances of religious salvation. For others still, it was a playground, a place to shelve their morals, and to indulge their every whim.

Many 'missionaries' made their way to the East End to do something about the condition of the people there. Some were motivated by religion, such as the Reverend Billing, who, as well as being a member of the Board of Guardians of the Whitechapel Workhouse, was a familiar figure in the Victorian press at the time, venting his rage at the slow progress of change in living conditions. Others might be those with more political motivations, such as Clara Collet, one of the contributors to the magnificent work on the Victorian poor compiled by Charles Booth. She lived amongst the people she wrote about; her commitment was to understand, catalogue and publicise the dreadful lives of the women of the East End.

Miss Louisa Twining, who features in much of the literature about the Poor Laws and the management of the workhouses in London, devoted her time to the improvement of those less fortunate than her, but her standard of living was completely unaffected by those she sought to help. Margot Asquith recalled in her autobiography the months she spent in Whitechapel in the autumn of 1888, visiting some girls who worked in the Cliffords factory there (and went with her 'girls' to visit the place where Mary Kelly died: 'the girls and I visited what journalists called 'the scene of the tragedy'. It was strange watching crowds of people collected daily to see nothing but an archway'.). David Lloyd George also took it upon himself to visit Whitechapel in 1888, to 'see to the bottom of things', while clearly enjoying the *frisson* of seeing such degradation at first hand.

There were innumerable prostitutes and brothels, and many dark alleyways and side streets where the prostitutes could see to their customers if they could not afford a bed. The availability of flesh of all ages and of both sexes for the gratification of those with money was shocking to many visitors in those days, and firmly puts paid to the idea that Victorian London was a prim world of crinolined maidens and covered piano-legs. It was only in 1885 that the Criminal Law Amendment Act raised the age of consent for girls to 16; before then, prostitutes as young as 12 were commonplace on the streets of the East End. And this was a violent world, too; 'one of the greatest problems of the police in the bad old days,' recalled Walter Dewin his memoirs of his time as a detective in 'H' division, which covered Whitechapel, 'were organised gangs. Lawless characters banded together, and under some fancy name went about robbing and blackmailing honest tradesmen, assaulting innocent pedestrians, garrotting and fleecing drunken sailors, and preying upon the defenceless foreign element, chiefly poor Polish Jews.'

Things were not really any better when the police were around and, in Flower and Dean Street, where the majority of brothels and lodging-houses were, even the constables would only walk in pairs. 'A single constable would have been lucky to reach the other end unscathed,' wrote Dew.

Despite the best efforts of the officials and leading citizens of Whitechapel, the East End was regarded as no less corrupt than the rest of London. In 1888 a parliamentary committee enquired into allegations that the authorities in London – the Boards of Guardians, the Boards of Works, and the various parish vestries – were spending ratepayers' money to fight reform. Complaints against maltreatment by the Master of the

Whitechapel Workhouse, Mr Thomas Babcock, were frequent, mirrored only by the routine nature of the rejection of any such complaint by the Board of Guardians and their seniors, the Local Government Board. It was only for the offence of fiddling the accounts or – as in the case of one assistant doctor – caustically rejecting the opinion of the Board, that an employee of the workhouse and infirmary need fear for his job.

Into this environment, the arrival of Jack the Ripper caused dramatic changes to the slums, their surroundings, and the people who lived there. Indeed, in the last few years it has even been suggested that the killer was motivated partly by the desire to provoke public indignation at the scale of the poverty and filth amongst the people who lived there. It takes but a glance at the photograph of the mutilated body of Mary Kelly to reject this notion.

The Whitechapel Infirmary is no longer there. When the Poor Law reforms were superseded by changes in the early 20th century, the workhouse system ended and the infirmary was turned into St Peter's Hospital. The hospital was later badly damaged by bombing in the Second World War, and was therefore demolished rather than being transferred to the fledgling National Health Service.

William Vallance, an extraordinary mine of information about the workings of the Poor Law, was a stickler for detail and nowhere is this better illustrated than in the entry he made for the fortnightly meeting of the Board of Guardians for 25 December 1888, when he notes, 'There were no guardians present; and entry of the fact is accordingly made pursuant to Article 32 of the Order of 24 July 1847.' It was Christmas Day, after all.

Vallance's work is recorded in the vast dusty volumes available at the London Metropolitan Archive, and in the form of submissions to his superiors at the Local Government Board at the National Archives in Kew. Photographs of the old infirmary, now demolished, are on various websites, as well as plans and elevations in books at the British Library. It was a forbidding looking place: one designed not to inspire as a sanctuary but as a place to dread. Its layout from these plans and from the notes given at its meetings can be imagined and, most importantly, (from a note written by the Clerk in 1889) we learn that the 'existing mortuary and Post-Mortem Room is not within the curtilage of the Infirmary, but at a distance of some 300 yards there from'. This is important because it meant that whoever was in that room – presumably not one visited often – was effectively invisible at night to the infirmary officials, and that he or she could come and go as they pleased.

The workhouses were brought into being through the efforts of parliament; under the terms of the 1834 New Poor Law, they were designed to bring to an end the excesses of public spending on poverty in any given area of the country. The cost of establishing and building them was borne by the creation of unions of parishes, and their management was overseen by local guardians of the poor. Within 20 years of their taking over the care of the poor, the workhouse system was the largest civil organisation in the country, having 700 institutions.

In order to receive assistance, however, poor people had to be overseen; they were to live in the workhouse, and they had to give up all their personal belongings and any effects that could be sold to pay for their upkeep. This meant of course the breakup of houses, and the separation of families. Called 'bastilles' by the poor, they efficiently imprisoned the sick, the unemployed, the disabled, the insane and the elderly, all at a rate that made the taxpayer happy. The workhouses were the epitome of thrift and Victorian philanthropy.

Life within the workhouse infirmary was not happy. So many detested the workhouse that it was inevitable that they sought to subvert its rules and regulations whenever they could, whatever the result. Maltreatment by those in authority who thought it their right to lord it over the poor was one problem; corruption and abuse were also rife. Bad behaviour was frequently marked out as requiring fierce punishment. Failure to do your 'work' – for example chopping wood or unpicking jute – could result, if you were a young man, in three months' hard labour. Even to be fed was something of a privilege. With unrelenting efficiency, William Vallance laid out the dietary table made for the regular inhabitants of the infirmary:

Breakfast 5oz bread 1/2oz butter 1 pint tea
Dinner 4oz cooked meat (5 times a week) 8oz potato or other vegetable (5 times a week) 3oz bread
Once a week: 14oz suet pudding Irish stew
Twice a week: Pea soup
Supper 4oz bread 1/2oz butter 1 pint tea

In the mid-1860s, the editor of the *Lancet* regarded the infirmaries of the workhouses as so disreputable in terms of the health and care they offered that he referred to them as 'antechambers of the grave'. Thanks to the efforts of one doctor, Dr Joseph Rogers, who stood up to the board of his infirmary, and who was determined to improve the reputation of the infirmaries, usually working against corrupt and bureaucratic boards, the infirmaries within the workhouses were gradually improved. The *British Medical Journal*, in its obituary of Dr Rogers in 1889, said of his efforts: 'Dr Rogers has turned over the stone of ancient abuse, and has shown the world...the vermin that throve in the darkness. As might have been expected, there was a mighty squirming and wriggling.'

So much is clear from what we can read about John Williams's public life. But there remains one problem; you are not going to get much private work if you kill some of your patients. It was all very well working in a large public hospital, but even there the chances were high that you would be risking more than the life of your patient. You might be losing a reputation that you were trying so hard to build up. Far better to do what had been done for centuries now; that is, take time to practise your work, and on those who would not – could not – complain about it. After all, such patients were going to die anyway if you did nothing. John Williams was neither the first doctor to think this way, nor the last.

John Williams was already used to charitable work, and to work far removed from the private surgeries of Harley Street. Not only did he work with servants and other members of the working classes in the hospital, but he also dealt with the impoverished at the dispensary attached to the hospital. This was still a bit too close to home for him, however, and the man who had been brought up to enjoy a more robust way of life than those cosseted middle and upper classes in the West End was not afraid to spend time with the indigent poor of the East End. He was hardly alone in this; when his friend Dr Herman of the London Hospital gave a paper to the Obstetrical Society in

October 1881, on the 'Relation of Anti flexion of the Uterus to Dysmenorrhoea', he had used a base of 110 women as his evidence; of these, 68 were East End prostitutes. These were women who could not get medical help except if it was offered to them; the best they could hope for would be a bed in the infirmary, where three hundred other women would compete for the attentions of one medical officer and his assistant, and hope that the supply of drugs had not been cancelled on cost grounds that month. Of course, they would be only too happy to comply with the wealthy, distinguished doctors who came along and offered them assistance, and the possibility of relief from their pain, even if it meant they had to put up with something awful. They had no prospect of any other kind of help. Into such a world, 'a hotbed of disease' with the 'moral atmosphere as tainted as the material,' wrote the *Pall Mall Gazette*, John Williams would have been welcomed with open arms.

Visits to the infirmaries of the East End workhouses by well-off people from the western side of the city were common. The Whitechapel Workhouse Infirmary has a visitor's book: alongside well-meaning ladies, there were the odd names of unexpected visitors, including officers from the army. Perhaps this was similar to the larger hospitals and asylums, which were open to curious members of the public for people to visit; the story of the visitors to Bedlam, the hospital for the insane, is well known, and maybe other hospitals and infirmaries were also on the tourists' route. What can be said for sure is that when well-off and important visitors such as John Williams came to the infirmary, they would have been welcomed.

What would John Williams have seen when he first visited the infirmary? What would life in the workhouse have been like, not only for its patients and inmates but also for staff such as Dr Ilott? We can piece together from the records held at the London Metropolitan Archives, and at the National Archives, something of the conditions. We can add to this from the reports carried in the local newspapers of the time, and we can refer to memoirs from those who stayed in the institution, such as the American writer Jack London, to give us a more vivid and personal picture than we are shown by the official records.

I have found that it is not easy to get into the casual ward of the workhouse. I have made two attempts now, and I shall shortly make a third. The first time I started out at seven o'clock in the evening with four shillings in my pocket. Herein I committed two errors. In the first place, the applicant for admission to the casual ward must be destitute, and as he is subjected to a rigorous search, he must really be destitute; and four-pence, much less four shillings, is sufficient affluence to disqualify him. In the second place, I made the mistake of tardiness. Seven o'clock in the evening is too late in the day for a pauper to get a pauper's bed.

For the benefit of gently nurtured and innocent folk, let me explain what a casual ward is. It is a building where the homeless, bed less, penniless man, if he be lucky, may casually rest his weary bones, and then work like a navvy next day to pay for it.

The first thing that becomes clear is that this was a place run on strict Victorian ideals of charity; the poor were not to be too well looked after, or they might become complacent and rely on the workhouse to provide them with shelter and food. The accommodation that was offered to them was only to be sought out of necessity, and not because it was convenient or saved a relative some money. The records show that those who were able to pay for the upkeep of their elderly or sick relatives, yet who sent them to be cared for on the parish's bill, were tracked down and made to pay. Non-payment was always treated as a great crime, just as the fit and healthy young people who found it necessary to stay in the workhouse were punished severely if they neglected, or avoided carrying out, their work. There was no punishment meted out by the courts, but there was a moral undertone to all the actions carried out by the workhouse staff and the guardians who ran the place. This is not to say that they themselves always acted well; apart from the corruption that seemed endemic within certain unions, as the groups of parishes were called, they were very harsh. Poverty, for them, was a moral stain, and no unnecessary kindness was to be offered to those who were foolish enough to be afflicted by it.

Occasionally, one or other inmate would decide to complain – whether it be about the bullying, as they saw it, of an old woman, or the confiscation from an old man of his few possessions.

Their complaints were inevitably aired by the guardians, but almost always dismissed; these gentlemen wanted to be seen to be doing the right thing, but rarely issued reprimands to their staff for activities that appeared to be about keeping the poor in their place. Every month, a local government inspector would call and report on the numbers of patients and inmates within the workhouse walls; he would also record the names of those men and women who had been taken before the magistrate for misdemeanours such as neglecting their work.

The Whitechapel Workhouse Infirmary was an enormous place. In 1889, Dr Herbert Larder, who replaced Dr Ilott as the Medical Officer of the Infirmary when Dr Ilott resigned in 1886, wrote to the guardians about plans for enlarging the building. It was already treating over seven hundred residential patients every day, and for this there were 90 officers, including all the stokers, washerwomen, cooks, and scrubbers, as well as the medical staff, who numbered merely the medical officer, and his assistant, together with the nurses who worked on the wards.

The medical staff in the infirmary were massively overworked, and they would have been only too happy to welcome a specialist into their midst who would relieve them of some of the work – particularly a specialist such as John Williams, who knew a lot about the conditions that so many of their women patients suffered from.

As we waded through the papers of the workhouse, two further clues revealed his presence in the infirmary. The first was the arrival of a nurse, Ellen Phillips, who had worked for the last four years at University College Hospital. UCH was a large institution (although *The Medical Directory* does not specify how many patients came through in any given year, the entry shows that it had the same large numbers of trained doctors as hospitals such as Guy's and the London, both of whom list over sixty thousand patients annually), and there would have been many nurses there, but, given John

Williams's appointment 'In Charge of Beds', it is highly probable that she would have known him, at least enough to wish him good evening. Ellen Phillips was appointed in 1886 to the position of night nurse.

Her character notice, sent to the Whitechapel Guardians by Sister Cecilia at UCH, says she 'was a good nurse and managed the wards and her patients well, but I was forced to dismiss her on account of her constant untruthfulness'. Despite this slur on her character, she was retained by the infirmary matron, who thought well of her, and her appointment was confirmed to the Local Government Board at the end of 1886 when the matron reported, through the ever-vigilant William Vallance, that Ellen Phillips was 'kind, attentive, patient, obedient and truthful as far as I can judge'. Ellen Phillips remained a night nurse until 11 June 1889 when she resigned. During her time at the infirmary, she was paid initially £18 a year, a sum rising to £22 about a year before she left (compared to the £18 paid to 'J. Williams' in the autumn of 1885).

Also interesting is the length of her stay – over two years – in the infirmary, at a time when the Board of Guardians was concerned about the turnover of nurses: particularly night nurses, whom they always found hard to attract to the job. When Deborah Gough, a night nurse, resigned in April 1888 after only a few months, she wrote that she was quitting her job because 'the matron does not wish the nurses to be at all comfortable'.

She went on at some length about this, in a sub-mission to the guardians:

'I was left on a Block by myself for seven weeks and also for shorter periods with patients dying on each floor besides young babies to attend to and when a patient has died through the night I have been obliged to walk and get another patient to help me lay the body straight and put the large screens around the bed.'

A compliant, familiar night nurse, grateful for her job, such as Ellen Phillips, would have been very glad of the knowledgeable assistance she received from a doctor she knew to be eminently respectable. He would probably have remained too aloof to have been much company for her, but at least she would have been assured of some professional guidance and support during his late night visits. Perhaps this is why she stayed in the job for longer than Deborah Gough.

A more personal view of a workhouse came from the pen of John Law, who wrote, in 1889: 'The Whitechapel Union is a model workhouse; that is to say it is the Poor Law incarnate in stone and brickwork. Doubtless this Bastille offers no premium to idle and improvident habits, but what shall we say of the woman, or man, maimed by misfortune, who must come there or die in the street?'

Within this atmosphere, the autocratic, determined and well-to-do doctor from the West End of London would have fitted in very well indeed.

Here was an institution devoted to the poor, in the district where the women who were killed were among the very poorest. Was it possible that there would be some link between these women and the infirmary? The only official connection we had come across so far was that the body of Mary Ann Nichols, the first victim, ended up in the Whitechapel Infirmary when it was taken to the mortuary after she was found on the street.

Perhaps by then John Williams had left for the West End, and home; perhaps he busied himself elsewhere in the infirmary? We do know that the initial assumptions of the police would have excluded him automatically. Abberline, the Detective in charge of the case, wrote about the murder of the second victim, Annie Chapman, and the claim that the killer was a man who knew her, one Edward Stanley. He said that it would not be right to be suspicious of him as 'he was a respectable hard-working man'. With such ready assumptions, who would challenge a high-ranking doctor such as John Williams?

In Whitechapel, we stood where the old infirmary buildings had once housed all those sick and dying people. We walked to all the murder sites, timing the trips. Even on a busy afternoon with everyone scurrying along to get out of the cold air, it did not take long to walk briskly from the infirmary to each of the murder sites. Durward Street – where Mary Ann Nichols was found – was less than two minutes away, with the places where Annie Chapman and Mary Kelly died not more than a five- or ten-minute walk. The murder site furthest away from the infirmary was that of Catherine Eddowes, at nearly fifteen minutes, but of course this was also a convenient distance from the place where, on the same night she was killed, Liz Stride died; convenient, that is, in taking the killer away from the hue and cry that arose once Liz Stride's body was discovered. We knew that in the early hours of the morning the streets would be a lot less busy, allowing the murderer to move quickly down the dark alleyways, and return to the sanctuary of the infirmary.

It was possible now to place John Williams at the infirmary, with a written connection to Mary Ann Nichols; then Annie Chapman and Catherine Eddowes and Liz Stride, who both had recorded entries in the infirmary's records. Surely this meant that our deductions were correct; the first four victims were in Whitechapel in the infirmary, and the doctor was there alongside them.

There was one vexing question about the victims and one that remains crucial: *for what reason* had they been killed? We did not feel that the Ripper was a sadistic murderer, as so many other solutions suggested – the women were all killed *before* their bodies were mutilated – but there was something about the women themselves that prompted the man to kill them. John Williams wanted something specific from them; these women were not picked out at random to die. At the time, some people thought this was a possibility too; one writer to *The Times* of 26 September 1888 said he thought that the killer could not be 'a drunken loafer' but was more likely 'a person making research from motives of science or curiosity'.

John Williams himself wrote that: 'The best scientific work does not meet with an immediate visible and palpable reward'.

The doctor would have looked at these women as nothing more than cases to be examined, symptoms to be understood, greater knowledge to be sought. He encountered them in the course of his work at the infirmary, and something about them – or maybe about their diseases – drew him to them. Knowing what he spoke about at the Obstetrical Society meetings, what he wrote his papers about, what he was researching, will give us an inkling of what exactly interested him about them so much.

We went through the papers that we had collected which dealt with John Williams's published work. His research papers show that he had chosen to focus on the uterus, its functions, and the diseases it was prone to. We already knew that he was remembered in the medical world chiefly for his use of abdominal operations, so we can assume that he chose to investigate the uterus and its complications with both surgical and internal examinations.

But why did he need to go further with the women who died at his hands, and what did he expect to learn from them that he could not have learned within the walls of the infirmary?

He wanted something specific from these women, and we believe that what John Williams wanted more than anything else was to understand the function of the ovaries, their relation to fertility, and to see if he could perhaps use the organs he removed from the women to complete his research. Maybe he even wanted to go so far as to transplant these fertile organs into his sterile wife. We have no evidence of this, but it is a distinct possibility, given the remarks of Dr Matthews Duncan, the President of the Obstetrical Society, who said that he used to think curing sterility was impossible but had lately come to the view that it was 'sometimes cured'.

I had read a news report recently that two Swedish women had been the first in the world to get a uterus transplant…the very procedure that John Williams had strived for all those years ago and now it was amazingly possible. Did the doctors who had achieved this technique know of the work carried out by Dr Williams? Did they refer to his papers and medical studies he had carried out back in the 1880s?

CHAPTER NINE

I looked again at the reports of the victims' lives, and decided to work methodically through all I knew of them. To start with, the investigations were easy. Mary Ann Nichols, it was widely noted, had spent most of the last few years of her life living in workhouses, mostly in Lambeth, for she featured often enough in the records of the institution there. It was because the name of the workhouse was stitched into her undergarments that she was identified in the first place. Besides that, she was named by John Williams himself in one of his notebooks. So far, so good. However, Annie Chapman did not appear to have been to the infirmary, though she did use a variety of names, as did many of the women. Annie was involved in a fight about three days before she died and declared then that she was going to go to the infirmary to seek treatment.

The infirmary records deposited at the London Metropolitan Archive include the admissions and discharge books for 1888. As you might imagine, these have been heavily studied over the years, and it is now no longer possible to see the volume for the second half of 1888. It is being restored, and, because of the backlog of materials, this may well take years. Although I was not able to see for myself if Annie Chapman's name (or any of her pseudonyms) showed up in that book, to date no other accounts of the Ripper's crimes mention finding her name in that or any other workhouse records.

There is another possibility. Not only do we know that people turned up at the infirmary and refused to give their names – as happened in 1884, for example, when questions were asked in the House of Commons about the role of the workhouse – but we also know there was a back entrance. It is through this entrance that John Williams might have left the premises, unobtrusively, to walk the streets. Again, the records are clear that there is a back entrance because during 1888 20-year-old Edward Maloney escaped through it. Security within the workhouse premises was never particularly good – as the sad example of Betsy Wilks who burned herself to death showed. So is it possible that Annie Chapman was able to gain entrance to the infirmary without having her name recorded? She had pills on her when she died; she spilled them and collected them up in a scrap of paper, which led to two innocent soldiers being questioned about her death. She must have got these pills from somewhere; given that she declared she was going to the infirmary, it is impossible to believe they came from anywhere else.

In the lists of people up in front of the magistrates for various offences at the workhouse, the name 'John Kelly' appeared a number of times. Kelly was the lover of Catherine Eddowes, the third victim. Catherine herself appears in the records of the infirmary under one of her surnames, which she had taken from her first lover and the father of her children, Thomas Conway. She was inside the infirmary, for a 'burn of foot', on 14–20 June 1887. Her address was given as a house in Flower and Dean Street.

But there was another, more intriguing connection with Catherine Eddowes that I came across early on in our researches, and which I tried hard to track down. When we read the *Transactions of the Obstetrical Society of Great Britain,* I noted the firm relationship I could establish through its pages between John Williams and his two friends, Dr Champneys and Dr Herman.

Dr Champneys, because of his father – and we felt there was likely to be a family connection with Dr A.M. Champneys – could already be linked to Whitechapel. Dr Herman, like Dr Francis Champneys, was a friend of John Williams, although the two men appear never to have worked at the same institution together – at least on paper. However, they collaborated on papers for the Obstetrical Society and I can see that Champneys and Herman were strong supporters of John Williams when he was pressing his case or, indeed, when he was made President of the Society. Under his presidency, the two men became joint Secretaries to the Society. The fact that the three men worked together on their papers was noted by the *Lancet* in the 23 June issue, 1888. But the key thing about Dr Herman is that he worked at the London Hospital – and that he took patients, and, in late 1887, one patient in particular, from the hospital where Dr Champneys and John Williams both worked, the Lying-In Hospital in Waterloo. And what was particularly fascinating about this patient? She was suffering from a disease of the kidneys known as Bright's disease, an inflammation of the kidneys now known as nephritis.

Catherine Eddowes was suffering from Bright's disease, and Eddowes was the victim whose mutilation included not only the removal of part of her uterus but also her kidneys. It was supposedly her kidney that was posted to George Lusk, the chair of the vigilante committee in Whitechapel.

When I read this, I wondered what I had found. John Williams had made a special study of Bright's disease when he was training to become a doctor – it was possible to see this when looking through some of his medical notebooks in the National Library in Aberystwyth. But when I started to look for evidence that this woman – unnamed by Dr Herman – was Catherine Eddowes, we found nothing, and she remained anonymous. However, just as I was about to give up my search, and admit to failing to find a connection between her and the infirmary, she turned up in the Admissions and Discharge book from the workhouse infirmary. As with Annie Chapman, I looked for her under some of her other names and there was Catherine Conway, in the infirmary, in 1887.

Catherine Eddowes had tattooed on her arm the initials of the father of her children: TC, or Thomas Conway.

So now I had traced the link between Mary Kelly and John Williams. I also knew that Polly Nichols had seen John Williams, and that Annie Chapman and Catherine Eddowes had been patients in the infirmary at one time or another. This left me with Liz Stride, and every account we read of her life states that she was living in the infirmary during 1881 when she was suffering from bronchitis. This was obviously much earlier than any of the connections with the infirmary that I had so far been looking into, but I do know that John Williams had been associating with Dr Ilott from the infirmary since 1877.

So what sort of person was John Williams? It is difficult to establish what kind of character he was. He was a good host for his fellow doctors, entertaining them at his club; he was firm and unyielding in his opinions, and this sometimes rubbed up people the wrong way. Not enough is known about what went on inside his head, and as he had taken pains to remove pages from the 1888 diary (which, until the pages were removed, was filled more substantially than all his diaries), nothing can be gleaned from these sources. Remarks he made in passing indicated that he barely tolerated people he considered beneath him, in terms of their intelligence and capacity for hard work, but no more could be deduced than this.

Equally difficult to ascertain is the true nature of his relationship with Mary Kelly. The fact that the relationship had rocked his marriage enough for it to be recalled a hundred years later meant that it had obviously been an important one. We know that it was enough to take Mary away from everything she knew – including her child – and so it was more than just a passing fancy for both of them.

If John Williams was a doctor who killed, even if he felt these deaths were necessary in the cause of his research, was he any different from doctors who kill because it gives them some kind of thrill? Was it possible that he had killed before 1888 – that his victims died on the operating table, rather than on the street, and that instead of being castigated as a criminal he was hailed as a pioneer? Would the women who died under his knife – and there would undoubtedly have been some who did – have felt themselves to be victims any the less if they knew that their deaths were going to enable other women to live? And if he, Dr Williams, allowed himself to think like that, would he have worried about a few sad old prostitutes who were almost certainly going to die in a miserable way in the next few years anyway?

But what if all the victims were linked not just in death but also in life by their killer? Suppose that first Liz Stride, then Mary Ann Nichols, then Catherine Eddowes, then Annie Chapman, all came before John Williams in his role as doctor during his time at the infirmary? We know that Mary Ann Nichols did; we know that the other three women were all in the infirmary at some point. And suppose that the final victim had inadvertently been selected long before, several years ago, when she had made the mistake of taking up with a rich doctor. We are not suggesting that John Williams had planned the murder of these women over many years; merely that the women (who – apart from Mary Kelly – all looked about the same age as his wife) made the mistake of being the wrong patients, in the wrong place, at the wrong time.

No one who met him in the streets outside the workhouse infirmary in the autumn of 1888 was ready to question Dr John Williams about his presence in Whitechapel. The doctor was a regular fixture at the infirmary; provided he had no other reason to be at home or out of town he would turn up at the infirmary.

Sometimes he would spend long hours there, into the night, carrying out the research he could not do earlier in the week on account of his other commitments. Perhaps he kept working then because it kept him away from the home that increasingly depressed him. His determination to do something about his wife's condition, as well as to make his name, must have increased as the years went by; his failure to do anything for her or for himself must have become increasingly difficult to bear.

So, a demoralised, overworked Dr Williams willingly takes himself away from his home to visit his occasional clinic in Whitechapel one August evening. Whitechapel is bustling day and night; being close to the docks there is a constant need to provide food, drink and other necessities to the thousands of visiting sailors and dockyard workers. Dr Williams arrives in Whitechapel to find it as busy as ever; he becomes anonymous in the crowd, a familiar sight over the last eight-or-so years. He is not accosted by the streetwalkers; they know he is not looking for their custom. They recognise him as someone who has been as intimate as any paying customer, but, unlike those men, his interest in them is not for sexual gratification. By comparison, his interests seem almost altruistic. Perhaps one or two of them stop him to tell him about their illnesses; perhaps they know only too well that it is this aspect of their bodies that truly animates him. Maybe he even recognises one of them, Polly Nichols, who came to him a few years ago with a baby, and left without one? Does she smile at him? Does she exhibit the same signs of an early pregnancy, signs that only a doctor could see?

Does he feel angry to think he left his fine but barren wife in their fine but empty home, only to come here to see some fecund whore flaunt her pregnancy at him?

He walks through the infirmary this August evening; the staff there change with alarming frequency, and after the many years he spent alongside Dr Ilott he has found it easier to go straight to the separate building, housing the mortuary and the post-mortem room, where he keeps his research jars and instruments, rather than spend time with Dr Larder, the officious new doctor in charge of the infirmary. He settles himself, and begins to calm down. So what if Polly Nichols is pregnant? What does that matter to him? Unless what if he could learn something from this? What if Polly, who is probably dying of some disease or other anyway, could be parted from her womb, so that his wife, a much more deserving case, could benefit? After all, women had died before by his hand; women who were nearly dead anyway, but whose life expectancy, instead of being lengthened by surgery, had been radically shortened. No one had missed them; who would miss Polly Nichols?

We do not know what John Williams did now; had he seen Polly earlier in the evening and arranged for the two of them to meet later? Did he know long before then that he was going to have to kill someone, to keep his research alive?

When he had done so, what use would the parts of their bodies he removed be to him? How did he manage to evade notice and capture when all of Whitechapel was out hunting for Jack the Ripper? And, most importantly of all, what convinced him to stop committing these crimes?

The police were in every nook and cranny of Whitechapel by the time of Mary Kelly's death; Queen Victoria herself had written to the Home Secretary to express her worries about the on-going situation in the East End. The police had visited the infirmary; Inspector Abberline wrote in September about visits to 'the London Hospital and other places', but had to admit that 'no useful information has been obtained'. Vigilante groups roamed the streets and alleyways at night; the area was unsafe for almost any single man to walk through, as he would be set upon by the mob, and only if he was lucky be turned over to the police. John Williams knew it was no longer a safe place for him to visit. The evil that he had done and the monomania that had foisted it upon him caused him to have a breakdown that took him away from UCH and his other duties. After taking no part in any of the meetings for the months of October and November with the Society of Obstetricians, John Williams returned to the meeting in early December but made no further presentations of papers – then, or ever again.

So if these are among the reasons John Williams stopped committing the crimes, what was it that caused him to start? We have assumed that he saw a woman he knew and that something about their shared past – the fact that he had helped her when her child had aborted – meant that he knew she had the ability to reproduce, and understanding of this is what he craved.

Something drove him to think that a woman of this kind – in her forties, fertile – would have the answers to the problems he was facing. And when this Polly Nichols did not, he was driven on to find others, others that he knew about, any one of whom could have held the secret that he longed for within the confines of her body. A kind of mania overtook him, and he no longer saw them as alive but as people he knew were sick and dying – albeit slowly – and whose deaths might benefit the lives of many, many more.

Dr John Williams was never Jack the Ripper. Jack the Ripper never existed; his name, as is well known today, was coined by two newspaper reporters (the police believed them to be the authors of some of the supposed Ripper 'letters' as well; many letters were written by hoaxers, including one woman, who was arrested in Bradford), and, although they never accused them, they suspected Tom Bulling of the *Central News*, and his boss, Charles Moore, of being behind the creation of the dreadful name. The reporters knew only too well that the story of the killer roaming the streets of Whitechapel was too good an opportunity to miss. 'Jack the Ripper' became the name given to the killer by the newspapers because, then as now, a killer with a name like that sold papers. Dr John Williams was never the Ripper of public legend because he did not set out to sadistically kill for some kind of sexual pleasure – all of the women were strangled and their throats cut *before* any mutilations took place – and because he did not seek to create the kind of panic and terror on the streets of Whitechapel that ensued from the killings. John Williams was a doctor, a surgeon, and as such used to the touch of death in his hands; but he was not a man who was prepared for the furore that the killings brought about.

The countless women that had passed through his hands since he became a surgeon would have meant little to John Williams, other than those with the potential to improve his lot, either through their wealth and position in society, or those from whom he could gain medical insights. The ambitious man would not have cared about the women in Whitechapel except for what they could give him, and what he could learn from them. For the vast majority of the inhabitants of London, the lives of a few prostitutes were a matter of complete indifference to them. To John Williams, they would not have mattered at all. When the police visited the workhouse to question the staff and the inhabitants about the killings, as we know they did, they would not have been suspicious of the well-to-do doctor, even if he had been present – the staff in the infirmary would not have brought him to the attention of the police because he had been coming to the infirmary for years before the murders started.

No one believed that the killer was anything other than a deranged maniac, and probably a foreign one to boot. Only the more thoughtful members of the police doubted this: Inspector Abberline, speaking some fifteen years after the murders were committed, said, 'You must understand that we never believed all those stories about Jack the Ripper being dead, or that he was a lunatic, or anything of that kind. No; the identity of the diabolical individual has yet to be established, notwithstanding the people who have produced these rumours and who pretend to know the state of the official mind.' Whereas another account wrote: 'It was in accordance with current belief in British pride and moral superiority that no Christian Englishman could have perpetrated such abominations; therefore it *must* have been a foreigner'.

There were innumerable prostitutes and brothels, and many dark alleyways and side streets where the prostitutes could see to their customers if they could not afford a bed. The availability of flesh of all ages and of both sexes for the gratification of those with money was shocking to many visitors in those days, and firmly puts paid to the idea that Victorian London was a prim world of crinolined maidens and covered piano-legs.

The doctor had settled upon his victims; they were women he saw around the streets of Whitechapel, and women whom he had at some point examined. He knew something about them and what they could offer him, so they were not going to be frightened of him when he approached them – particularly once the whole district was awash with people who had set out to capture the Ripper, or at least to frighten him off. Apart from the vigilante groups that had formed, men came to Whitechapel with the aim of catching the killer or understanding the women he preyed upon. One man dressed up as a woman, hoping to entice the Ripper; instead he was chased by a mob who thought he was the killer. Another, a doctor, dressed in 'a jersey in place of a coat, his face most palpably artificially blacked' – a disguise that fooled only the mob who chased him into the arms of the police. If Polly Nichols, or Annie Chapman, or Catherine Eddowes, or Liz Stride, was approached by Dr John Williams, they would not be frightened at first – here was someone they knew, someone they trusted. They would not have balked at moving away from the busy streets and going into dark alleyways and small yards with him, even at a time when they knew the risks. He was a doctor, he had been there for years; what could possibly go wrong? Policeman Walter Dew wrote:

'Let us assume for a moment that he [the killer] was a man of prominence and good repute locally. Against such a man, in the absence of direct evidence, it is too much to expect that local police officers would hold such a terrible suspicion. And, assuming this to be the case, the man's amazing immunity can be the more readily explained. The same qualities which silenced the suspicions of his women victims would keep him right with the police officers who knew and respected him.'

Then something more interesting about his attendance times showed up. In 1889, the hours at which he saw in-patients changed; he continued to see women during the week, now on Tuesdays and Thursdays at 1.30 p.m., but he also added 9.00 a.m. on Saturday mornings to this list. Perhaps he wanted to make it difficult for himself to be elsewhere at those times; perhaps he wanted to have a ready excuse for no longer attending a voluntary clinic elsewhere. It seems a good explanation. His private practice had grown during his career, thanks no doubt to his appointment as physician *accoucheur* to Princess Beatrice, and at this stage he would have been expected to cut back on his working hours in the hospital, not to increase them. And yet he had done so, and *at the weekend* in particular; surely an even more concrete indication that this was a man who had used his weekends prior to 1889 for something that he did not want widely known.

Going back further in the minutes of the meetings of the hospital's medical committee reveals more of his working life there.

John Williams had to list his annual holiday dates for the committee, and he took a long time off – usually two months over the summer – though, as this was not remarked upon in the notes, perhaps there was nothing unusual in this. In the meeting of 25 January 1888, John Williams told the committee that he had handed over to Dr Spencer all his teaching duties, as he now had 'care of beds' under his authority instead. It is probable that this was a managerial role requiring him to hold regular meetings at the hospital, presumably less onerous than standing in a lecture room in front of medical students. The minutes of the management committee through

1888 show that the hospital closed that summer 'for drainage alterations' for five weeks, so Dr Williams's holidays were extended that summer. In addition, the attendance notes for the committee show that John Williams was not present at any of the committee meetings that autumn until a meeting on 12 December, which he only attended in order to make a case for employing a third assistant in his department to deal with out-patients. In the following year, 1889, Williams attended every meeting, including one on 10 July, at which his request for new hours (involving him working on Saturday mornings) was approved. He continued to attend meetings far more regularly than he had in 1888, and at the end of the year was voted Dean of the Medical Committee.

At the end of the following year, in the meeting of 17 December 1890, John Williams told the committee that he wished to be 'relieved of the duty of performing ovariotomy'.

He was relinquishing *exactly* the operation carried out by the Ripper on the streets of East London on the bodies of Annie Chapman and Catherine Eddowes, and which the murderer was assumed to have tried out – but had not had the time to complete – on the other victims, Polly Nichols and Liz Stride.

So within two years of the dates of the Ripper's crimes, John Williams had altered his working hours so as to tie himself down more to UCH, and to cease performing the operation that had made the Ripper such a notorious and feared killer; two substantial leads linking him to the crimes.

One last record – in 1891, John Williams stepped down as Dean and did not appear on the minutes again until he announced his retirement. He did not appear to resign from the hospital in the same way as Dr Graily Hewitt – no letter was read out at the meeting, and although Dr Williams, like Dr Graily Hewitt, was appointed Consultant Obstetric Physician (with Dr Spencer promoted into his place), none of the usual courtesies in their addresses to the meeting from the other members of the committee were afforded to Dr Williams on his retirement.

The early and abrupt departure of John Williams from the place that had given him his first job in London, and where he had trained, was puzzling. The official history of University College Hospital, noted that, 'Williams retired from the active staff of UCH in 1893, having for some years in fact handed much of his work, including abdominal operations, to his successor Herbert Spencer'. It also said that Williams retired prematurely, on the grounds of ill health: John Williams retired at 53, but during the remaining 33 years he managed to establish a national library – hardly the sign of a man who was suffering unduly from illness.

To summarise: John Williams had worked at UCH from 1872 through to 1893. During 1888, he had limited his hours to weekdays only, leaving the end of the week and the weekend free; only in 1889 did he reverse this and ask to work on a Saturday morning. He also sought to further reduce his workload at the hospital in 1888, giving up teaching; and in 1890 he had asked specifically to be relieved of the operation that had made the Ripper notorious. It seemed as if John Williams had worked at the Eastern Dispensary, covering for his friend Dr Oldham, and that he had ensured that he had the time away from UCH to carry out his work there. When he stopped working in Whitechapel, he put temptation behind him by making it impossible for him to leave UCH at the weekends, and then stopped carrying out the specific operation that was a reminder of his crimes.

At some point, then, Mary Kelly travelled up to London, perhaps in the company of John Williams. She was said by a newspaper of the time to be living in Knightsbridge; according to some, she was in a house in Cleveland Street. A man named Edmund Bellord claimed to have found Mary Kelly a job in the street there, working in a shop. Cleveland Street lay midway between Queen Anne Street, where John Williams and his wife lived, and UCH, where he worked. The street would not have been more than a five-minute walk from either his home or the hospital where he worked – placing her very close to him indeed.

Perhaps he was determined to keep her near him; maybe that is why she moved into a house in a street halfway between his home and the hospital where he worked. The points of connection between the two of them are such that it seems unlikely to be just a coincidence – firstly, the link in Cardiff, and then living less than five minutes from him in London.

That would make sense; if you want to be with someone and if that someone had left their family for you, you would want them near you.

This must have suited the doctor to have Mary close, but not too close for comfort. Was it him that decided she should work, making sure she didn't get any ideas that could potentially spoil his agreeable home and work environments? Or maybe Mary didn't want to be a kept woman, she must have had some pride and dignity left. Whatever the case it seems this scenario suited them at the time.

CHAPTER TEN

M ary Kelly was the Ripper's final, and most mysterious, victim. She was a young widow and, according to her lover Joe Barnett, fairly quickly after her husband's death she became a prostitute. An Irish girl in Wales; a woman from South Wales; a country girl once in London, perhaps even a working-class girl in the company of a rich man? It is not surprising that we cannot find much evidence of her life, only that of her death. She continues to exert a fascination on all those who study the Ripper's crimes because of two irrefutable facts: her youthfulness and attractiveness when compared to the other victims, and the terrible assault on her dead body.

We went about searching for information to corroborate the testimony of Joe Barnett given at the inquest on Mary Kelly's death. As it summarises the only known facts about her, it was the obvious place to begin. Although some of the facts were corroborated by a newspaper report published in the *Star* of 12 November 1888, a few days after her death, the *South Wales Daily News* of 14 November 1888 was unable to verify any of the details given in Joe Barnett's testimony. If it had proved so hard to check the facts when she had just died, it was going to be very hard for us today to get a clear picture of Mary Kelly's past. No one has come close to finding out enough about her background to convince anyone that they had found the 'real' Mary.

Some of the most famous theories have even suggested she was the reason why the Ripper killed in the first place. Why? Because she was different in almost every way from the other victims. She was younger, by some fifteen to twenty years, and she was prettier. Inspector Abberline, who headed the Ripper investigations, had been in Whitechapel's H Division for 14 years. He would have known by sight many of the women in the area, and would have agreed with the view held by the police at the time that she was 'possessed of considerable personal charms'. She was a prostitute like the others, but the story of her life before, and her rapid fall from respectability to the slums of Whitechapel, was swifter and sadder as a result. She was also, unlike the other women, young and attractive enough to be able to leave this environment and change her life, as she had done before. She died in her own room. The other victims died in the street. Her body was appallingly dismembered and disfigured, more so than any of the other victims. This showed one crucial difference in the murders; the killer had allowed himself time with her, as he no longer had to cut her up quickly out on the street. Did he choose her as his final victim in part because he *could* take his time?

Joe Barnett's words at the inquest to the coroner were transcribed by the clerk to the court in language probably very different from that of Barnett, who was a porter at Billingsgate fish market. This is one reason to doubt the veracity of everything he is reported to have said.

She said she was born in Limerick, and went when very young to Wales. She did not say how long she lived there, but that she came to London about four years ago. Her father's name was John Kelly, a 'gaffer' or foreman in an iron works in Carnarvonshire, or Carmarthen. She said she had one sister, who was respectable, who travelled from market place to market place. This sister was very fond of her. There were six brothers living in London, and one was in the army. One of them was named Henry. I never saw the brothers to my knowledge. She said she was married when very young in Wales to a collier. I think the name was Davis or Davies. She said she had lived with him until he was killed in an explosion, but I cannot say how many years since that was. Her age was, I believe, 16 when she married. After her husband's death deceased went to Cardiff to a cousin.'

The Coroner: 'Did she live there long?'

Joe Barnett: 'Yes, she was in an infirmary there for eight or nine months. She was following a bad life with her cousin, who, as I reckon, and as I often told her, was the cause of her downfall.'

The Coroner: 'After she left Cardiff did she come direct to London?'

Joe Barnett: 'Yes. She was in a gay house [a brothel] in the West End, but in what part she did not say. A gentleman came there to her and asked her if she would like to go to France. She said she did not like the part, but whether it was the part or purpose I cannot say. She was not there more than a fortnight, and she returned to England, and went to Ratcliffe Highway.

Barnett then went on to give details about his first meeting with Mary Kelly, and their life together. The report from the *Star* mostly corroborates what Joe Barnett had to say, but there are some additional details that are useful to note. It reported that she called herself Marie Jeanette Kelly after her trip to Paris, and some of the writers of the time follow this conceit. Returning to her initial arrival in the East End, on Ratcliffe Highway, the report continues:

'Her father came from Wales, and tried to find her there; but, hearing from her companions that he was looking for her, Marie kept out of the way. A brother in the Second Battalion Scots Guards came to see her once, but beyond that she saw none of her relations, nor did she correspond with them. The authorities have been making inquiries concerning the soldier who, according to Barnett, was in the Second Battalion of the Scots Guards. That regiment is now in Dublin, and it is understood that inquiries will be immediately prosecuted there'.

If there was a resolution to this inquiry, nothi[ng] been recorded; nor is there any indication in the Home Office papers now in the National Archives that anyone was sought in Dublin in connection with Mary Kelly's death.

The *Star* report continues: 'It has been stated more than once that Kelly was a native of Limerick, but a telegram received from that place last night says that inquiries made in that city have failed to identify the latest Whitechapel victim as a native of the town'.

There is little doubt that Kelly came to London from

Cardiff some five or six years ago, leaving in that town her friends, whom she has described as being well to do. She is stated to have been an excellent scholar and an artist.

It was best to take these reports – of Mary Kelly's talents with the brush, and her sobriety – with a pinch of salt; from reading all of the reports into the lives of the murdered women, as recalled by their friends and relatives at the inquests, it is clear that no one wanted to speak ill of the dead. All their good points were exaggerated, and their bad ones overlooked, but this made piecing together the truth about Mary Kelly's past that little bit harder. The *Star* had more detail to print about Mary Kelly's first experiences of London:

'It would appear that on her arrival in London she the acquaintance of a French lady residing in the ourhood of Knightsbridge, who, she informed er friends, led her into the degraded life which has brought about her untimely end. She made no secret of the fact that while she was with this lady she drove about in a carriage, and made several journeys to the French capital, and in fact led the life of a lady. By some means, however, at present not exactly clear, she suddenly drifted into the East End.

Here, the area that Joe Barnett roughly identifies as the West End is named as Knightsbridge. We believed the report that Mary Kelly was installed in Cleveland

Street, but even if this were incorrect, she would not have been a five-minute stroll from John Williams's work or his home, but only a little further off in the opposite direction. Knightsbridge, after all, would be only a 10-minute ride away by Hackney carriage or horse-drawn omnibus. The remarks about her swiftly descending to the East End led us to assume that her 'supporter', the man providing her with the income to live in such luxury, suddenly withdrew his financial aid and she found herself hastened across town as a result. This also suggested to us that the man had sufficient influence to ensure that she was made to leave behind any opportunity of making money in the West End, so that he would not have to come across her again. Unless, of course, he chose to. This demonstration of his power might account for the fact that Mary Kelly never told Joe Barnett who her 'gentleman' was. She knew the risks if she were to identify him. The *Star* reports:

Her first experiences of the East End appear to have commenced with Mrs Buki, who resided in one of the thoroughfares off Ratcliffe Highway, now known as St George's Street. Both women went to the French lady's residence, and demanded Kelly's box, which contained numerous costly dresses. From Mrs Buki's place, Kelly went to lodge with Mrs Carthy, at Breezer's Hill, Pennington Street.

This place she left about 18 months or two years ago, and took up her quarters in Dorset Street. As to her ever having a child, the testimony is conflicting. Mrs Carthy declares positively that she never had one. Mrs Carthy states that the deceased when she left her place went to live with a man who was apparently in the building trade, and who she (Mrs Carthy) believed would have married her.

It appears from inquiries made at Carmarthen and Swansea that after leaving the former place for the latter, Kelly, who was then only 17 years of age, entered the service of a Mrs Rees, who stands committed to the next assizes on a charge of procuring abortion, and who is the daughter of a medical man formerly resident at Carmarthen.

This last, intriguing line seems to be nothing more than a red herring in the report, but the connection with the 'medical man' is of interest. Was it the product of an overactive imagination, either on the part of the journalist or the person he spoke to? Or did Mary Kelly have to provide some kind of cover story one day to Joe Barnett, when she let slip that there indeed 'a medical man' – a doctor who had come from the valleys of Carmarthen – in her past?

The data had been collected orally, as there were high levels of illiteracy in Britain at that time. (Mary Kelly was illiterate and used to ask Joe Barnett to read to her from the newspaper.) The census-takers recorded the information by hand, and it remained in that form until transcribed many years later by the Mormons. The census was taken then, as now, every 10 years and so could not only identify people in their homes but also show in later years how life had changed for them; how many children joined the household, who within the family died, and exactly how many servants they may – or may not – have had.

Like *The Medical Directory*, the census records were to prove invaluable to us. The records for Swansea showed that there was a John Kelly living in the city in 1881 – although he did not have a daughter called Mary living with him. We knew from the estimates of her age when she died, 23 to 25, that she would have been around 15 or 16 during the census of 1881.

It was a disappointment that we could not find her on the sheets that identified 'John Kelly', born in Ireland but living in Swansea, and we seemed to have reached a dead end. But when a breakthrough came some weeks later it was in answer to a different question and from an unexpected source.

If a connection between John Williams and Mary Kelly could be proved, their common Welsh background would probably provide the key. The census surveys for South Wales in 1881 were interesting but ultimately unhelpful. There were Kellys alright, even a Mary Kelly in Swansea of about the right age, but her marriage certificate clearly revealed it was not her.

According to Barnett, Mary Kelly's large family included seven brothers, a sister, and a father named John employed as foreman in an ironworks in Carmarthen or Carnarvonshire. These and other details that Barnett gave, under the pressure of the coroner's inquest, were specific. For us to track her down, given the scepticism with which we felt it was right to treat the details that Barnett gave, was going to be difficult if not impossible.

The ironworks, however, provided another interesting angle. We knew that Richard Hughes, the father of John Williams's wife Elizabeth, was a wealthy entrepreneur with interests in mining, steel, tin and iron. One of his factories was the Landore Tin Plate Works near Swansea. Could there be a connection between the Hughes family and Mary Kelly's father John, in his role as foreman of a South Wales ironworks? Much has been written about the industrial heritage of South Wales, but it was just our luck that the employment records of the Landore Tinplate Works had been lost. If the Kelly family were involved in the business – if the father was foreman of the works – then the proud Richard Hughes would have presented his new son-in-law to his key workers. Perhaps the son-in-law would be shown round the works and thereby meet Mary, the foreman's young daughter?

However, we were sure Mary Kelly's family had moved on long before that. We reasoned that she had left home when young to marry the colliery worker, Davies, and that when she had drifted into prostitution after his death she had effectively cut all her ties with her family. Perhaps they did not want to acknowledge her as their child once they had read about her dissolute life. Maybe they did not recognise the 'Marie Jeanette Kelly' that the papers wrote about. Maybe, after her father died in 1883, the family had returned to Ireland and never knew what became of her. It was worth returning to the documents that gave details of John Williams's time in Wales. The chances that the doctor met Mary Kelly in London were too slim. Their paths might have crossed in Wales; in London, where she lived initially only a few minutes' walk from both his home and his place of work; or in Whitechapel, where she died. It would have to be in Wales, from everything we knew about her family history. He met her there, took her to London and to Paris with him, and then he abandoned her.

We thought it highly likely, especially when we took into account the likelihood of Joe Barnett's testimony based on conversations with Mary Kelly being many months before and only hazily recalled.

Joe Barnett said that Mary Kelly had told him her family had lived in Carmarthenshire in the south, not in the north.

In at least one report on Mary Kelly after her death, it was noted that 'it was thought there was a child' from her marriage.

I decided to look closely again at Joe Barnett's statement to the inquest, and with the benefit of everything we had now uncovered, confirm or refute what he had said:

1. She said she was born in Limerick, and went when very young to Wales.
2. She came to London about four years ago.
3. Her father's name was John Kelly.
4. He was a gaffer, foreman, in an ironworks.
5. She said she had one sister and six brothers, one in the army.
6. One of them was named Henry.
7. She said she was married at 16 to a collier, Davis or Davies.
8. She lived with him until he was killed in an explosion.
9. She went to Cardiff to a cousin.
10. She was in an infirmary for eight or nine months.

For a while, maybe she was everything Dr John Williams wanted – young, compliant, pretty and lively. There is even a rumour that she spoke Welsh as he did. At some stage, then, he went one step further than simply visiting her in the house where he had installed her; he took her to Paris. A few short years later, when she was in Whitechapel, she told Joe Barnett that she did not like it there and came back to London, but perhaps the truth is that John Williams did not like it there with her; that he realised what a fool he was being with his young mistress, while his wife was alone at home in England. So they returned to London, only for him to abandon her. Without her protector, she was forced to leave the comfortable house she had been living in, in the heart of wealthy and privileged London, and start on her downward path to the East End.

I couldn't make any sense of this information. Parts of it sounded like Mary Kelly, or what I'd been told about her, but everything else was as though it was written about somebody else. I needed to look into the family tree and find out exactly what was true and what was either fictitious or simply written about another person.

The Mary Kelly Joseph talked about was an enigma; he only knew what she chose to tell him of her past. Her name wasn't her own…she hid her true identity from all those around her. All he knew is what she wanted him to know; not a lot added up with her story, it was as though she had taken pieces of other women's lives in order to make up a past for herself...how much of it related to her we'll never know.

I know that Mary came to London to be with John Williams and that she had also travelled to Paris with him. Had he abandoned her; forcing her to live in the grim, seedier side of London with her friend? She would no longer have had the means to pay for something more decent.

Was Dr Williams that cold; surely he knew what she had given up for him, the sacrifices she had made? Would he have left her penniless and destitute? Something wasn't adding up, I wasn't sure what, but I would find out.

CHAPTER
ELEVEN

Meanwhile, John Williams perhaps decided to make something of his life with his wife, and maybe they renewed their attempts to have children. Perhaps the previous efforts to do so were now overshadowed by his experience of the rather more worldly Mary Kelly; maybe his disappointment in his wife became more pronounced. It seems commonplace to deride Victorian marriages as fine on the surface, and a hotbed of secrets and recriminations underneath, but it would appear that this was the case with Dr and Mrs Williams. All the evidence points towards an unhappy union for both of them and, from what we know of his personality, there is no doubt that Lizzie was made to feel his disappointment more acutely than John Williams felt hers.

But maybe there was something else which has not made it into any official records. John Williams's researches, as we discussed in relation to the interests shown by the papers he delivered at the society he had joined, now focused intently upon the function and diseases of the uterus. If he believed that his wife's apparent infertility came from her having suffered from one of these diseases in the past, maybe his increasing scientific interest was coupled with a private desire to seek a cure for her. The doctor would have paid more regular visits to the infirmary in Whitechapel; the sick lay in such numbers here that he was always able to find exactly the kind of patient that matched his wife for age and general condition. Although the murdered women were, with the exception of Mary Kelly, older than Lizzie Williams, newspaper reports from the time state that they appeared younger than their actual age – perhaps making it clear why the doctor selected those particular women, and not some of their equally miserable fellows.

The doctor would have looked at these women as nothing more than cases to be examined, symptoms to be understood, greater knowledge to be sought. He encountered them in the course of his work at the infirmary, and something about them – or maybe about their diseases – drew him to them. Knowing what he spoke about at the Obstetrical Society meetings, what he wrote his papers about, what he was researching, will give us an inkling of what exactly interested him about them so much.

No one who met him in the streets outside the work-house infirmary in the autumn of 1888 was ready to question Dr John Williams about his presence in Whitechapel. The doctor was a regular fixture at the infirmary; provided he had no other reason to be at home or out of town he would turn up at the infirmary.

In his memoir, Detective Ben Leeson, a man who joined the police force around the time of the murders, wrote: 'Amongst the police who were most concerned with the case, there was a general feeling that a certain doctor, known to me, could have thrown quite a lot of light on the subject. This particular doctor was never far away when the crimes were committed and it is certain that the injuries inflicted on the victims could only have been done by one skilled in the use of the knife.' Perhaps the police suspected more than has ever been known; but their suspicions could not be made into evidence against their suspect.

Walter Dew's words show that the police were not far off the mark. The killer was spotted once; at least, it is thought that one of the witnesses who claimed to have seen the killer was genuine. George Hutchinson knew Mary Kelly and saw her on the night of her murder with a man whom he described as about thirty-four or thirty-five, 5'6" in height, with a moustache, a long dark coat, and respectable in appearance. He also mentions a red stone on the man's coat.

John Williams's friend and colleague, Herbert R. Spencer, wrote about the doctor and the way he used to dress in London, in an article which appeared after the Welshman's death. He describes him as he knew him in London in the late 1880s: he was of middle height, robust build, he usually wore a frock coat, silk hat, stand-up collar and a dark silk tie held by a pin set with a red stone.

Once in private, John Williams immediately killed the women by strangling them and then slitting their throats, which meant that they could not cry out, and that they did not bleed profusely on to him. The fact that most of the wounds were seen to be cuts from left to right suggested to many that the killer was left-handed.

The statue of John Williams in the National Library in Aberystwyth shows him holding the plans for the library in his left hand. However, it is more likely that the killer stood behind his victims, perhaps following them into the place they suggested for their assignation, and strangled them and cut their throats from behind. This would have the double benefit of surprise as well as keeping their blood away from him.

The knife used in the murders was, according to the

doctor Thomas Bond (who carried out the post-mortem on Mary Kelly), 'of the same character' in all the murders with the exception of Liz Stride's – the assumption of many writers is that the haste with which the Ripper acted in her case means there was not enough evidence for Dr Bond to state it was the same knife.

It was 'a strong knife, at least six inches long, very sharp, pointed at the top, and about an inch in width'. It may have been a surgeon's knife, he said, but 'I think it was no doubt a straight knife'. This is the knife in John Williams' possessions, held in the National Library of Wales. I am sure of it.

The library's listing of two of the items contained in these boxes is on page 301 of their catalogue of John Williams's archive. It simply states, 'Knife with black handle' and '3 microscopic smears in small wooden box'. Until we can go into the library with the right equipment, and the right experts, we cannot be certain what these items will do to our case.

These two items from that box have gripped our imagination more than any others. The slides, wedged under tiny slivers of glass, contain what is very evidently animal – rather than plant – matter. More than that, we cannot say. Alongside them in the box is a wooden-handled knife, about six or so inches long. It is difficult to be more sure than that because the tip has snapped off. The knife is old, but it is not a kitchen knife, or a garden knife; the blade widens just after leaving the wooden handle to about one inch or so before tapering down to the point. It is still razor sharp.

Why would you keep such a knife? Surely such an eminent and wealthy surgeon would have gone through many, many knives and scalpels in a whole career of performing operations?

Why keep this one in a collection of what were mainly documents? What made it so special, considering it was so battered and well used? And why would he keep such a thing when he had given up practising surgery so many years before? Is it possible that, on the knife, there are any traces remaining of what it had once cut?

And those slides. Why, after a professional career spanning decades, were those three slides there, among the final artefacts of this man's life? Would the slides not be more use in the teaching hospital he worked in? What possible use could they have for him? And, if we were able to examine them under a microscope today, what could they show us? Would it be possible to determine whether or not it was human material under that glass, and from what part of the body that material had come from? Was it from a woman? Would it be possible to prove something with it?

To hold the knife in your hands as John Williams must have held it is a chilling moment.

I am in no doubt as to why he kept this knife. Perhaps for years it had sat harmlessly in his desk drawer for him to cut string, but we believe it had a use well before that time. *In every respect,* this knife matches the one described by Dr Thomas Bond.

Using this knife, after the murders, John Williams would have been able to carry out the mutilations to the bodies, obtaining from them what he wanted. Given the nature of some of the mutilations (leaving aside those to Mary Kelly), and the speed at which they were carried out, taking into account the darkness and the prospect of discovery at any moment, it seems unlikely to us that the killer could be anyone other than a doctor. The police did look at this possibility, and medical students throughout the capital were examined with a view to establishing whether or not they could be the killer. One newspaper carried reports of a doctor from Birmingham being arrested at Euston, but no follow-up to his arrest exists. Senior doctors such as John Williams were not considered suspects. They were respected members of society, usually Freemasons and therefore known to their fellow Freemasons in the police and judiciary; they were people of standing in their community who could not possibly commit crimes of this kind. We are less likely to take this point of view today, and yet we are still shocked when doctors such as Harold Shipman are shown to be serial killers. Who would, then, back in the 1880s, have suspected a man such as John Williams?

Mary Kelly was by far the youngest of the other victims, the prettiest, and she died in her own home. Why did John Williams kill her? Was she a greater target than the other women because she had tempted him – or was it because she was some kind of threat to him? Could she have identified him? In her last few days, according to Joe Barnett, she was very frightened of the Ripper and asked Joe to read to her from the newspaper about him. Did she suspect him? Had she seen him, at night, walking along with one of the women who later died? And why, when she died, did he defile her body in the way he did? The sight of her corpse is horrific – but does it look any different from any other body dissected by a student in a hospital?

We wondered whether there was any link between the apparently mindless destruction of Mary Kelly's body and the religious element of John Williams's life.

Whether it was some kind of signal to fellow masons it is difficult to know. If the killer was acting with these thoughts in his mind, then he would have to know the appropriate passages from Leviticus and what they meant very well in order to recall them while engaged in such vile slaughter. Bearing in mind that John Williams was the son of a preacher, and had been brought up by his mother to enter the priesthood himself, he most certainly would have known his Bible.

We compared the two passages:

'And he shall bring his trespass offering unto the Lord for his sin which he hath sinned, a female from the flock...for a sin offering.... And he shall bring them unto the priest, who shall offer that which is for the sin offering first, and wring off his head from his neck, but not divide it asunder....And he shall offer the second for a burnt offering, according to the manner: and the priest shall make an atonement for him for his sin which he hath sinned, and it shall be forgiven him.' (Leviticus 5: 6, 8, 10)

The 'manner' is specified in Leviticus 7: 2–4:

'In the place where they kill the burnt offering shall they kill the trespass offering: and the blood thereof shall he sprinkle round about upon the altar. And he shall offer of it all the fat thereof; the rump, and the fat that covereth the inwards. And the two kidneys, and the fat that is on them, which is by the flanks, and the caul that is above the liver, with the kidneys, it shall he take away.'

Mary Kelly was a prostitute; was she a 'trespass offering'? At her inquest, the following details were revealed:

The body was lying naked in the middle of the bed…The whole of the surface of the abdomen and thighs was removed and the abdominal cavity emptied of its viscera. The breasts were cut off, the arms mutilated by several jagged wounds and the face hacked beyond recognition of the features. The tissues of the neck were severed all round down to the bone.

The skin and tissues of the abdomen from the costal arch to the pubes were removed in three large flaps. The right thigh was denuded in front to the bone, the flap of skin including the external organs of generation, and part of the right buttock. The left thigh was stripped of skin fascia, and muscles as far as the knee. The pericardium was open below and the heart absent.

As we know, in the room where she died there were traces of a large fire in the grate, so hot that it had melted off the spout of a kettle. Her heart was missing; and was never found. Though the ashes of the fire were carefully sifted, according to the press reports, no sign of human remains was discovered. We cannot rely on the rumours that abounded in the press at the time, but no other theory sufficient to explain the excessive heat of the fire has been put forward.

One thing is irrefutable: her mutilation went far

beyond that of the other women. Of course, it could be argued that this fate only befell her because the other women were killed on the street, and her killer had the space and time to carry out his work in private. But the reports of her death and the two photographs that exist suggest something deeper, something more personal, in the frenzied attack on her dead body. If, as we suspect, she knew John Williams, did she also suspect he was the Ripper – and was she planning to blackmail him? Was she going to expose him, as an adulterer – or even a murderer? Or was this a crime that had less to do with her and more with him; the killer wanted to make this the final murder, and the resemblance between her mutilations and the lines from the Bible was no coincidence but a ritual carried out to mark the conclusion – and to send out a signal to those who would recognise it, that the 'atonement' had taken place?

At some point, perhaps when he felt the police came too close to him, the sheer awfulness, the magnitude, of what he was doing must have overwhelmed him. He had been oppressed by the mutterings within the profession against him, as well as by the absence of children in his marriage. Once he had embarked on his murders in the East End, he could not stop until he had marked their end in some way – as the corpse of Mary Kelly and the way it had been mutilated indicated – and it was only then that he could confront the terrible realisation of what he had done.

John Williams temporarily settled back into his life of practising at UCH and, for a short while only, at a small number of other institutions. In 1893 he resigned from UCH and gave up all other kinds of work in public hospitals. For the next few years, he devoted himself entirely to the private patients that were going to help fund his retirement, and he continued to assist the Queen in attending the births of more royal children. The reversal of his enterprising and ambitious career is sudden. At the end of 1888, he is at the height of his powers; within four years, he had abandoned almost all his public work. He claimed 'poor health' forced him to retire from UCH, but he continued to practise privately and to work for the royal family for many years afterwards, and he was a tireless and vigorous campaigner for the National Library of Wales well into the next century.

Add to this the fact that he lived for another 33 years after his 'retirement' and the state of his health does seem a somewhat incredible excuse for retiring. Why this sudden decline in his work? Did he recoil from performing ovariotomies because the process reminded him too clearly of what he had been doing in Whitechapel? Did he retire from UCH and the other places in which he worked because he no longer wanted temptation, in the form of poor and compliant women patients, to be placed before him?

In 1903 John Williams retired from private work and moved to the coast beyond Swansea, to the village of Llanstephan. This village nestled in its own little cove while on the hill behind it sat a castle, and the 'magnificent mansion', as the local guidebook calls it, of Plas Llanstephan, which is where the 'Royal Surgeon' (also from the guidebook) Sir John and Lady Williams lived. It was in Llanstephan that the flowering of his wealth and power showed itself, while Aberystwyth represented his twilight years, with the great achievement of the National Library of Wales behind him.

He was a presence within the village, chairing parish council meetings to discuss important issues such as the sobriety, or otherwise, of the ferryman who worked out of the little harbour, or the matter of lighting in the village – a vexed issue that culminated with one meeting ending 'in disorder'.

Life in Plas Llanstephan must have been delightful. It was a large house, unchanged – at least externally – from the time that Sir John and his wife lived there through to the present day. The house, built in the second half of the 16th century and enlarged and rebuilt in the 1780s, is an imposing white mansion that sits on the hillside above the village overlooking the old castle on the opposite hill. It commands impressive views over the Towy estuary.

Such a large house seems a world away from the small farmhouse at Blaen Llynant, a powerful symbol of just how far he had come in life. Four servants, all women in their twenties, none of them from Wales, lived alongside Sir John and Lady Williams in the large mansion. In such a rural location, and set apart from the village, it must have seemed the perfect retreat for the doctor and his family. He was clearly putting all his London affairs gradually behind him, so much so that in one of the obituaries published many years after his death, the writer remarked that 'so renowned was his association with the National Library of Wales, that many men and women forgot the pioneering gynaecologist of the 1870s'.

From Plas Llanstephan, Sir John travelled up to London regularly for the General Medical Council meetings – although he had retired from all active duties in medicine, both public and private – but his life in London was over, and it was to this beautiful house that he would happily return. Here too he built up his large collections of Welsh manuscripts and printed books, adding to the already substantial collection he had started in London. In the bibliographic records of the

National Library, the bulk of these documents are referred to as 'the Llanstephan manuscripts', from where they were shipped up to Aberystwyth when the library was established. Here, at his rural home, he held the meetings with those who were also involved in the founding of the National Library – John Humphreys Davies, Dr Gwenogvyrn Evans and others.

The site of the National Library was an enormous issue in Wales, but Sir John would tolerate no opposition to his choice of Aberystwyth for its home. It helped that the land on which the library sat had been donated to the cause. His trump card against any arguments put forward by prominent citizens in Cardiff or Swansea was that he simply refused to send his collection anywhere but Aberystwyth. If the National Library was not there, he would simply send his collection, the finest in Wales, to the University Library in the town instead. His reasoning was a mixture of practicality and snobbery: Cardiff and Swansea would not do, because the readers at the library must have cheap living in the town available to them when they came to use the library's facilities. It must be somewhere where the casual passer-by would not drop in to read the newspaper and fall asleep in an armchair; and it must not be somewhere that tourists would just tick off their list of sights to see. More tellingly, he did not think that Cardiff's 'mongrel and non-Welsh population' (as he wrote in a letter to

J.H. Davies) would be the right people to look after his precious books and papers. The ill temper that characterised the debate over the home of the library culminated in editorials in the *Western Mail,* with statements such as 'it is Wales's misfortune that she cannot possess that library in the real sense of useful possession. At best it can only be hidden away in Aberystwyth,' or the council meetings reported that same day that accused Sir John of 'piracy' and his 'open antagonism to Cardiff'.

In the next couple of years John Williams made changes to his life that remained for the rest of his days. Once he moved down to Plas Llanstephan, he only returned to the world of medicine to attend meetings of the General Medical Council, and to help out at the birth of Princess Mary's children. The years in Harley Street, in Queen Anne Street and latterly Brook Street paid off, as he enjoyed a comfortable retirement and indulged himself in collecting the vast numbers of books that he was later to donate to the National Library of Wales. Of the years in Whitechapel, perhaps there were only a few small reminders; some microscopic slides, a knife, a letter or two, and the odd reminder in his papers, such as the notation of his meeting with the patient Mary Ann Nichols. And his diary for 1888, its pages carefully but systematically removed.

In June 1903 a banquet was held in Cardiff, at the

Royal Hotel, in honour of Sir John Williams, to mark his retirement and return to Wales. Present at the banquet were dignitaries from the city and from the surrounding area, among them many medical men. Perhaps most moving for the doctor was the presence of his old employer, Dr Ebenezer Davies, who not only came to the dinner, along with dozens of others, but also spoke in praise of his former employee. Sir John was pleased to especially thank Dr Davies, 'who had given him his start in the medical profession and bestowed upon him much valued advice'. I was putting together a clear picture of John Williams' life from the materials I read, and began to draft it into a kind of timeline so that I could start to make sense of what I had uncovered so far.

John Williams lived in Blaen Llynant with his wife, Lizzie, and with his mother-in-law, from 1910, once he had put his heart and soul into making the National Library more of a reality than a dream. With his three servants, this would have been quite a household, and the imposing house on the seafront would have been busy with callers and with business being attended to at all times of the day. Once he stepped outside, the retired doctor would have been able to look down the sweep of Marine Parade to the headland where the castle sat, and dream of the independence that it represented. For Owain Glyndwr's stand here – and that of the defenders who resisted the

Roundheads when they came to conquer the castle in the 17th century – was a rallying call for Welsh independence, a rallying call the doctor heard and tried to emulate in the symbol of Welsh culture and pride he was building on the hillside behind the town. In years to come, the castle's mixed lineage, Welsh and English, would be represented in the combination of symbols stuck alongside it. The standing stones within the castle walls, known as the Gorsedd stones, were erected in 1915, for the National Eisteddfod, but were eclipsed by the tall war memorial raised after the First World War, bearing the names of those from the locality who had died in that conflict and the war that followed some twenty years later. By then, of course, John Williams had faced his own tragedy; his wife, Lizzie, died of cancer of the rectum, as her death certificate states, in 1915. He was left alone in his home with his mother-in-law.

Leaving his front door behind, the doctor would make his way down Marine Parade. Aberystwyth had become a popular town in the late Victorian age, with bathing machines on the beach and a water-powered cliff railway, a favourite of Victorian seaside towns, away to his right. On top of the hill was a Camera Obscura, where the image of the outside world was reflected down onto a table in a darkened room. In John Williams's time in the town, by now the Edwardian age, he would perhaps have gone by car to the library at the top of the hill away to the east of the town. We know he travelled frequently in cars, though he never owned one, from the numerous taxi bills that sit in his archive in the library. Perhaps he would stop first at a hotel for lunch; as one of the town's more important figures, he was often hosting meals there, both for the library and for the university. This impression of importance was largely created by the doctor himself, of course, and he even took the trouble to send out copies of his portrait to a hundred people or so – including the bank, for example – so that no one might have trouble recognising him. From everything we read, John Williams had become more difficult than ever; quick to criticise his peers, troublesome with those who disagreed with him, and harsh on those he considered beneath him.

Once Lizzie had died, the warmth must have seeped out of Blaen Llynant. In one of the short memorial pieces that appeared in the UCH magazine after his death, John Williams's old assistant, Herbert Spencer, recalled visiting the doctor, who complained not of missing his wife but of missing his work – work he had been in such a hurry to turn his back on in the early 1890s.

But there was still work to be done when they first moved into the house on Marine Parade. The move from Plas Llanstephan in 1910 to Aberystwyth happened in time to oversee the building of the National Library. The building was begun with the blessing of John Williams's old friends, now King and Queen, George and Mary. The familiarity with which he had dealt with them in the past had now changed, and protocol demanded a different relationship with the Prince. Now the doctor had to write to the King's equerries, and every last detail of the King and Queen's trip to lay the foundation stones of the library had to be raised and queried, even down to the question of who was to be responsible for laying water on the road that the King and Queen would take from the railway station, so that the dust (should there be any) would not trouble them in their carriage. At this ceremony, the King also conferred upon Sir John Williams the honour of a Grand Cross of the Victorian Order – he had already received a Knight of the Victorian Order in 1902. Following his retirement, John Williams devoted the rest of his life to the National Library of Wales. The National Library was his long-held dream, and he was able to bring this to fruition through not only the political pressure he and other prominent Welshmen could bring to bear on the government, but also through the vast collection of Welsh manuscripts and early printed materials which he had amassed over the years. Sir John Williams died in May 1926. In his will, he left all his money to the National Library and to the University in Aberystwyth, and nothing to his family. 'The library ... will ever remain as the memorial of a far-seeing and single-minded man,' said the *Lancet*, in his obituary.

CHAPTER
TWELVE

Now I thought I knew everything I needed to know about John Williams thanks to Tony Williams's research; my next task was to find out about my great great grandmother, Mary. I knew she must have loved John; after all she had left her family in Swansea to be with him in London. Having a family myself I couldn't understand how a mother could leave her children… how did they feel? A child not knowing or understanding why their Mum had gone.

What did she tell my great great grandfather? How did he react? The whole family must have been devastated.

My grandmother had told me everyone was shocked by her leaving and it was the talk of the area for months…in a small community in Swansea secrets couldn't be kept for long, everybody knew each other and looked out for their neighbours.

Was Mary so in love she was oblivious to her family's feelings? Or could she be just as cold as her lover could be? There were so many questions to be answered...and I wanted to find the answers.

I needed to piece together the events that led up to the deaths in Whitechapel; what had happened so drastically to make someone like John Williams kill these poor vulnerable women. I knew he was trying to solve his wife's fertility problems...but surely he must have had some sort of psychosis to murder these women in the name of science.

Did my great great grandmother have any idea what he was up to? Was she with another man at the time? A lot of the evidence I had read through didn't add up to the story Nan had relayed to me, I had to unscramble this maze of paperwork and see if I could make sense of the written and the oral information I'd been given.

I tried to imagine what my great great grandmother must have thought when she arrived in London; there would have been a vast difference to the town she came from, and the smog-laden city she saw when she got there. She must have been in awe of London; the city was immense compared to Swansea and she would have surely felt intimidated by its vastness, lonely even, without her family around her. Was she distressed at leaving her children behind? Did she think that by being with John she would better her life and therefore better that of her children? Or was she just thinking of her own happiness…was she that callous and unfeeling? What mother would leave her child? This was something else that saddened me.

Her new found friend travelled with her to London; that must have been some comfort to her. She would have been apprehensive…but was she also happy and excited knowing that she was going to be with John? I wondered if she thought he was going to leave his wife for her…as many mistresses past and present do. Only to be let down time after time with empty promises.

My Nan told me that her great grandfather was a good man, kind and considerate, a man who thought deeply about things but never let things get to him. I suppose, sadly, he had learnt from experience after his wife had left him…he would have had to get on with things for the children's sake. Being a proud man, it must have taken a lot to put on a brave face when everyone was talking about how sorry they felt for him. I felt a sense of pride in him, he was someone I would have liked to have known, someone I think I could relate to; we seemed to have the same values and morals…he must have passed them down to me.

Some women, it seemed, were bored with a husband who was loyal and dependable and family orientated, a man who'd want nothing more than to make them happy. Instead, they always appeared to go for men who are egocentric and patronizing; the type of man who, as long as they were happy, wouldn't care about the 'mistress's' feelings. And yet for some bizarre reason it only made the women want them more.

What goes wrong in a marriage? As a couple they had been happy, had shared each other's lives, had laughed, loved, lived. They had made love and declared love, made plans, had dreams. Somewhere amongst all that they had lost it. Surely it was worth fighting for, if you had it once you could find it again. I know stresses and strains of everyday life can get you down, but you're the same person inside you've always been.

I had had friends who had done the very same thing, the pattern was identical. They knew their husbands were good and loving…but it was the lovers they proclaimed their love for.

I couldn't fathom out why you would give your heart and soul to someone knowing that it wasn't reciprocated. However, love is a strange phenomenon and I'm not here to judge what people should or shouldn't do…I just find it difficult to understand the reasoning for it.

It was funny to think that a story in a magazine had started me off on this journey of discovery: not knowing where it would take me or knowing what I would find out next. Nevertheless, the prospect excited me, the unknown lives of my ancestors coming out into the open. They had lived, loved and I was here because of them; I felt I owed them, at least to show who they were, why they did what they did, and what became of them.

Piecing the story together wasn't going to be easy, but I was going to give it a go and hopefully tell it as I found it. Some of it wouldn't be easy to relay, I would probably upset some family members, but then again the truth sometimes hurts.

Philip was very supportive, between my university degree and the family research, it felt as though my family life had been put on the back burner. Philip seemed to understand I needed to tell the story, not just because it was about my family but because it was it was entwined with the story of one of the most notorious killers in history.

I've been back to the local archives on numerous occasions, trying to piece my family together bit by bit. I've had my Nan to fall back on when I've been stumped by something that doesn't seem to fit; we go through the information and she just slots it into place. I didn't know she knew so much about our ancestors, but she's a mine of information.

Some days are long and laborious, sitting in front of a

screen for hours on end. Checking the censors, the marriages, the births and the deaths. It's a revelation when I find what I'm looking for and I'm elated; another piece of the jigsaw slotted into place. Then there are the days when I find nothing, zilch, nada. It's like an obsession now, a need to know, to find out what happened to not just Mary, but the rest of the family.

I can understand what attracted John Williams to my great great grandmother; she was a beautiful woman…quite similar to my grandmother in looks I've been told. Very classic looking with dark hair and dark eyes to match, she would have turned many men's heads. Was John jealous of the attention she received? Did his envy contribute to his breakdown, along with fact that he couldn't have children and my great great grandmother could and did?

What did she see in him I wonder…he was hardly a handsome man. His eyes, however, were deep and intense looking. He would have known how to please a woman I would assume; he studied women's bodies and their functions. He would have known all about the sensitivity of the vagina and how to stimulate it. Was their relationship based on sex? It must have played a big part. It seems odd thinking about the sexual activity of my great great grandmother, but I have to look at every aspect of their correlation.

His marriage seemed to have taken its toll on Lizzie

Williams; she had gone from a lively, happy woman, to an unhappy, down trodden doctor's wife. Their marriage was doubtless deteriorating.

She was probably aware he had had relationships with women or a woman outside the marriage, and that her continued inability to bear children provoked him. We believe this partly because she receives so little notice from him in the documents that survive, partly from the information that has been passed down the family, and partly from what we can detect from photographs of them at that stage in their marriage.

CHAPTER
THIRTEEN

So, after all this time, what had I found out? Well, we know that John and Mary did have an affair, which resulted in her leaving her family and moving to London to be with him. That I'm sure is irrefutable, the information fits in with the family story I've been told.

So what became of Mary and the rest of my family? This is what I've discovered.

Mary was born on the 4 September 1858…not in Ireland but in Swansea. Her father was a general labourer named Anthony who came from Ireland; I'm not sure what part…but I seem to remember my grandmother saying something about Galway. I've never been there, I've been told it's a lovely part of Ireland and I intend to go there soon, with my family. We will of course take Nan and my mother, who both want to see the place where all this started. Anthony married a local Swansea girl called Catherine and they had seven children: four boys and three girls. After all this time we still seem to be sticking with the family tradition of naming our children after our ancestors. I'm obviously called Antonia after Anthony Kelly…I also have an uncle called Anthony. Then there is Mary, there's a few of those in the family, not least my nan; Catherine, which is also the name of my mum, the list goes on.

Life must have been hard in those days; a lot of people had large families with very little money to support them. Nowadays people get shocked if they hear about young children working for a pittance in sweat shops and the like, as am I. But in those days it was a way of life…if you didn't work you didn't eat. Looking at my own children I can't even envisage them having to work until after they'd had a proper education. How times have changed…thankfully.

Mary married William in August 1879. What was Mary thinking about on her wedding day? That it should have been John she was marrying? Was she settling for William because she knew that John had married someone else? Or, did she love William at the time? I hoped it was the latter; after all she had children with him, that must have meant something.

Throughout my research I discovered that all the

family lived in the same area of Swansea, they never ventured very far. Some of the houses are still there today; obviously today they have been totally renovated beyond recognition of what they would have been back then. Did my ancestors own the houses they lived in, or were they just rented, which, if they were just labourers, I suspect was the case?

What was Swansea like in those days? It was obviously an industrious town, with its iron and steel works, it had the collieries and potteries. There was also the dock yard and port, quite evidently a bustling town. These days it's classed as a city. It was the town centre that John Williams had his surgery, the address is still there, although I wonder if it was rebuilt after the war, due to its current condition. His surgery was within walking distance to Mary's house, which my nan tells me was kept very neat and tidy. It was something her grand-mother told her numerous times, how house proud her mother was. That must be something else that runs in the family. Nan remembers her mother scrubbing the front step on her hands and knees, which is something you don't see today. The house would have been a small two-up two-down property close to the iron works and the town centre. I assume that John Williams's premises were a grander affair, with velvet curtains and expensive rugs and furniture. I wonder if he had given her any-thing for her humble home.

Where did John and Mary hold their trysts? Would it have been at his surgery, or would they have used one of the hotels in the town centre? The closest one would have been one of the Mackworth hotels.

The Wind Street Mackworth Hotel, which was quite grand and popular in its day; it was once run by a Mr Rotley whose son, Major Rotley, is celebrated as one of the famous men in Swansea, having served alongside Lord Nelson at the Battle of Trafalgar.

Nelson himself had stayed at the Mackworth when he had visited the town in 1802 along with the Hamiltons and as part of their visit they surveyed the Cambrian Pottery. Nelson's relationship with Lady Hamilton is well recorded, what may be less common knowledge is that 10 years after her lover fell in battle reports were received that she had died a pauper, in France, in 1815.

The 'Mackworth' of the High Street was equipped with 112 bedrooms and was a thriving part of town life within the vicinity of High Street Station. Youngsters before the war would warm themselves over the kitchen grills and would watch in awe as well dressed ladies and gents were led to the hotel entrance by the station porters, and gaze on enviously as they collected their generous tip. Occasionally they themselves would earn a gratuity by running errands for the staff, normally to fetch the latest edition from the platform book stands. The smell of the wonderful food used to breeze across the pavements and the once thriving hotel would be a very special spot for special occasions such as weddings and major functions. The Mackworth in the High Street stood until the 1970s and was one of the largest hotels ever to feature on Swansea's post-war skyline.

The other Mackworth Hotel disappeared from the town much earlier, having been acquired as the premises for the new post office, when it moved from Castle Street to Wind Street. Before its closure in 1898 the hotel wasn't without its scandal, in 1816 in one of the sumptuous bedrooms Fanny Imlay was found dead from an overdose of laudanum. Fanny was the sister of Mary Shelley, author of *Frankenstein*. Apparently, Fanny and Mary's husband Percy Shelley had been lovers before he eloped with Mary. Having received letters from Fanny, Percy arrived in Swansea but it was too late. He used his influence and had Fanny's name removed from her suicide note and declared 'dead' rather than a 'suicide' by the coroner. By doing this he saved her from being staked and covered in lime in the traditional crossroads burial of suicide. She is buried in a church yard on the High Street.

The information I uncovered while researching led me to the path that Mary took when she left Swansea to join John in London. After leaving her family she first travelled to Cardiff, where she apparently waited until

John had sent word to her. While there she made a friend, also called Mary; when Mary Kelly said she was leaving for London her friend asked if she could accompany her. Her friend wanted to get away from family problems; so Mary Kelly agreed for her to go. The new friend also asked if she could use her surname so that her family wouldn't be able to find her. Mary, not thinking it would be a problem, agreed…thus giving us two Mary Kellys.

Unfortunately, when they got to London John didn't take the same view, he had no intention of looking after the two women and so Mary's friend went her own way. What John didn't know at the time is that the two Marys kept in touch; Mary's friend, however, wasn't as fortunate to have a wealthy man to look after her and she had to live in the less than desirable area of Whitechapel, where her life took a downward slide into prostitution, like a lot of unfortunate women of that time. I can't imagine how it must have been to be in such poverty I'd have to turn to prostitution, but in those days there was no option women had to do whatever it took to even live day to day; there was no benefits system, just the workhouse, which would have been a last resort judging by what I'd read of them. Mary did all that she could to help her friend; she gave her what she could and often confided in her about her relationship with John. I don't know what their conversations entailed but what Nan had told me was that Mary's friend disliked John and the feeling was obviously mutual, when John found out about the girls' assignations he was apparently furious, he didn't like Mary mixing with a woman of ill repute. Even though he treated them in his professional standing to actually be involved with them socially was abhorrent to him.

What was said between the lovers only they will know, but considering what we know of John Williams I doubt he minced his words, it was probably a cold and hurtful altercation and hopefully Mary gave him just as much back, but I doubted that she would have stood up to a man like John, especially as he funded her lifestyle in London and she wouldn't have liked to end up like her friend.

Whatever took place, things seemed to take a down turn and started to cool off between them; what I've been told is that it was Mary who decided enough was enough and whatever John did or said couldn't change her decision, she had made her mind up. What had finally made her come to this resolve? She obviously loved him or she would never have given up her family for him. Something tipped her over the edge; had John started to get abusive or even violent? He had had some sort of breakdown, did this happen when Mary left him or had he shown some of these tendencies towards her and that's what had made her finish what they had?

My great great grandmother came back to Swansea just after the first murder took place, she moved back in with my great great grandfather who had decided to forgive her, which must have taken a great deal of courage, especially in the face of his peers who thought she had the audacity to think she could pick up where she left off. What did she say to him for him to welcome her home? He must have really loved her to put up with all the disapproving comments from his family and friends. Did she deserve his love? I don't think she did at the time. Nan said when she got back she was a changed woman, she seemed more nervous and unsure of herself, she had lost her strong will and resolve. Perhaps that's why William gave her another chance, he could see the woman he had married become a broken shell of her former self…she had become someone who needed looking after and his love was still strong enough to do that.

It took a long time before Mary would talk about her time in London, but eventually she told her mother about her experiences and her relationship with John. In the beginning he had been loving and attentive, bestowing her with gifts, taking her to theatres and out for meals. He had even taken her to Paris, which she found to be very exciting. But the last year they were together he had changed, some days he would snap at the slightest thing and blame her for anything that went wrong in either his professional or private life. He constantly told her she was worthless and no better than the whores that took money for their services. Other days he would be the man she fell in love with, apologising for his behaviour and begging her to forgive him…sometimes even breaking down and crying. He seemed confused at his own conduct, but couldn't stop himself nevertheless. Every time Mary said she was leaving he would get angry and he had slapped her on a number of occasions and even threatened to kill her if she tried.

I suppose, like many people in abusive relationships, both women and men think that they can change the person they are with, giving them chance after chance. It very rarely works out; if anything the situation becomes worse and the abuser gets more aggressive, probably because they think they will be forgiven every time. The abused will eventually reach a point where they can take no more, as was the case for Mary, and realise the only way it will stop is if they leave.

My great great grandmother had become scared of John and what he was capable of, so she had left him and told him she would never come back. This must have incensed him; he was the one with the money and power, he called all the shots. Was this his tipping point? His studies into fertility had come to nothing and now he was losing control over his mistress; it was obvious his state of mind wasn't what it should have been.

The Ripper murders were big news all over the country and when they read about it in Swansea they must have been surprised that the last victim was called Mary Kelly…not the Mary Kelly they knew, but what a coincidence. No one was more shocked than my great great grandmother; she must have had her suspicions but she had no proof that John Williams was connected to these abominable crimes. What she did know is that she had lost touch with her friend who was using her name, had she become the Ripper's last victim?

She certainly fitted in with the testimony and description that Joseph Barnett gave at the inquest of Mary Kelly. I can't help but wonder who this poor unfortunate woman was; she had used another name, 'Marie Jeanette', could that be a clue to her real name? She said her name was Mary, did she use Marie after my great grandmother came back from Paris and told her friend that the Parisians would refer to her as Marie? Perhaps she liked that take on her name better…but where did Jeanette come from? Was it her name or that of a member of her family? We will never know because we don't know what her surname was; she will forever remain an enigmatic figure.

It must have been hard for my great grandmother, she

was stuck between a rock and a hard place; knowing what had happened to her friend but not having any evidence it was John Williams who had committed the murders, she didn't even know her real name. How could she tell George, her husband, that one of the prostitutes killed was her friend...it was bad enough him accepting the affair she had without adding to the anguish by telling him she had suspicions of her ex-lover being the most wanted murderer in London.

So the secret she kept for the rest of her life, until her death in 1923, would only come out thanks to a magazine article over a hundred years after the horrific slayings took place.

All that remains is a silver locket which contains John Williams's picture; why did she keep it? After all that had happened did she still have feelings for John? Nan said she never wore the locket; it had been kept in a drawer in her bedroom. It had been passed down to her from her mother but she had never bothered to ask if the photo it contained was her grandfather, she just took it for granted, even though she had heard the story of the affair.

Mary had another child in 1889 who she named after her father Anthony; was he the result of a couple making up and proving their commitment to one another or was he possibly the reason that Mary had finally mustered the courage to leave an abusive relationship, knowing that she would never get away if he knew her condition? Again, this is something we will never know, but it is something we will always wonder about.